ABOU

The Decisive Event of Conversion

ABOUT TURN

The Decisive Event of Conversion

Peter Toon

HODDER AND STOUGHTON
LONDON SYDNEY AUCKLAND TORONTO

Bible quotations are taken from
the New International Version
unless otherwise stated.

British Library Cataloguing in Publication Data

Toon, Peter
  About turn : the decisive event of conversion.
  1. Conversion
  I. Title
  248.2′46   BV4916

  ISBN 0 340 41035 3

Hodder and Stoughton Editorial Office: 47 Bedford Square, London WC1B 3DP.

CONTENTS

For
Jack and Joan

PREFACE

In 1986 thousands of people have been celebrating the 1500th anniversary of the conversion of Augustine of Hippo to Christ and Christianity. Since he is one of my favourite theologians, I am very pleased that I have written this book on the occasion of this anniversary.

Augustine is claimed by Catholics as the great theologian of the Church and her sacraments: he is also claimed by the Protestants as the great theologian of the grace of God in Jesus Christ, our Lord. Bearing this in mind, I truly hope that what I have written on conversion will prove of value to both Catholics and Protestants. I wish I could say that Augustine, who is now with the Saviour in heaven, approves of what I have written! More importantly, I fervently hope that what I have said is pleasing to the exalted Saviour himself, before whom Augustine bows in worship.

I have written this book with my heart in my mind, with feeling as well as logic, in prayerfulness as well as in rationality. It is, I hope, what used to be called a contribution to *practical* theology and to *pastoral* practice. And it is intended for general readership inside and outside the churches.

My heart speaks loudest and with most passion in chapter ten where I plead for recovery of confidence in the Gospel, and in its *converting* power, within our churches.

I am most grateful for the support of my family, Vita and Deborah, and for the encouragement and help of David Wavre, a director of Hodder and Stoughton.

The book is dedicated to the Rev. Jack and Mrs Joan Whittaker, who are the godparents of Deborah. Jack is the Chaplain at Helen House, a hospice for children in Oxford.

Feast of the Transfiguration   The Rectory, Boxford,
1986   Nr Colchester.

1

GETTING STARTED

This is a book about conversion – turning to Jesus Christ. You may ask, 'What are your credentials for writing on such a topic?' and 'Do you know what you are talking or writing about?' Fair questions! I shall try to answer them.

Credentials

First of all, allow me to say that I have studied what the writers of the Bible have said about the topic. Further, I have read widely in the literature concerning conversion produced by Christians over the centuries. And I have carefully pondered what they have written. So from the point of view of study and scholarship, I think I have done my homework. My textbook for American colleges, entitled *Born again: a biblical and theological study* (Baker Book House, 1987), reveals some of that homework.

Someone may say – and I appreciate the observation – that head knowledge is one thing, heart experience/knowledge is another. So the further question arises, 'Do you know – that is, have you experienced – what you are writing about?' I must now attempt to answer this important question.

I cannot present you with any dramatic story of personal conversion, such as the story my wife told in the book *The Unexpected Enemy* (Marshalls, 1985) – the story of how a Muslim freedom-fighter became a committed Christian evangelist to, and servant of, the poor. Ghulam Masih Naaman had a momentous and hazardous journey of faith to become a disciple of Jesus. In contrast, my own story is much less interesting. In fact it is not unlike that of J. C. Ryle, the first Bishop of Liverpool, whose partial autobiography I edited and published in 1975.

Looking back over his life, Ryle could not point to any specific moment or day on which he felt he was born into a new life of union with Jesus Christ. But he could see that over a period of months in late 1837, when he was 21, there had been a great change in his life. He wrote:

> The circumstances which led to a complete change in my character were very many and various . . . It was not a sudden, immediate change, but very gradual. I cannot trace it to any one person, or any one event or thing, but to a singular variety of persons and things. In all of them I believe now the Holy Ghost was working though I did not know it at the time (*A Self Portrait*, p. 39).

There came a time, he said, when he knew he was converted; but that time came after a process which he hardly recognised at the time as a move towards conversion. He knew that by the grace of God he was converted because not only had he come to delight in biblical teaching but also to desire to know God personally as his heavenly Father and Jesus Christ as his Master and Teacher.

I left school at the end of the fifth form when I was 16. It was in the months following my ceasing to be a schoolboy and beginning to earn my own living that I came to accept as true the biblical teaching concerning Jesus and God's grace and salvation through him. In this period I came to desire to attend Christian worship, enjoy Christian fellowship and to seek to know God through prayer and biblical study. I find it difficult to be precise as to when this process/movement within me actually began and ended (in a sense, it has not yet ended): it was like being in a train that enters a tunnel and only being conscious that there has been a tunnel through the impact of the bright daylight streaming into the carriage at the end of it.

Like Ryle, I can point to a variety of factors and people through which/whom I believe the Holy Spirit acted to bring me to this point and to lead me on towards God through varied experiences. These include Christian teaching and example in home and Sunday school, certain books and the prayers of friends and family. Since then, over the last twenty or so years, I have been to many places, studied many subjects, and gone through a host of varied experiences: yet in all this time I have never seriously doubted that Jesus, Incarnate Son of God, is the Way, Truth and Life and that in him, and in him alone, is the only way to God, our Creator and Redeemer. I would now claim that while it is necessary to turn around to face Jesus Christ, it is also important that one walks towards him in faith, hope and love. In this sense, conversion is a continuing event throughout life, including high points of special joy and exultation.

As a minister of the Church of England, I clearly see the necessity of conversion for every person I meet, even for the kindest and sweetest. Ultimately, conversion is all about beginning to live in a right relationship with God, a life of faith, hope, love and obedience. Such a relationship is a gift of God to be accepted gratefully from him: it cannot be manufactured by religious machinery or pious activity. And I am happy that we use Service Books (the *BCP* and *ASB*) in this church which *often* emphasise the need for all to turn to God through Christ in repentance and faith.

I hope I have now said enough for my reader to give me the benefit of any doubt and to read on to discover what I have to say about this activity of God, producing in us that turning to him which we call conversion.

Potential readers

Let me now say for whom I think I am writing. Inside our churches I have in mind the busy pastor/minister/priest, those laity who are involved in the preaching and teaching of the Gospel as well as acting as counsellors, and any others who feel they want to know more about Christian doctrine and experience. Outside the active fellowship of the Christian congregation, I have in mind that growing number of people who are hungering after spiritual reality and truth; due to the failure of the Church they have tended to believe that they will hardly find that for which they long in Christianity. I hope they will look seriously at what is conversion to Jesus Christ.

Since the subject of conversion to God is most serious and thus deserving of our best efforts, I believe I can expect my readers to make a determined attempt to use every power of their minds to get to grips with the subject. I appeal to my readers to be patient with me and to follow the presentation carefully: I truly believe (I hope I do so modestly) that those who make the effort to understand will greatly benefit from their endeavours and thus be able to think more clearly for themselves about conversion to Jesus Christ.

Part 1 of the book attempts to present the teaching on conversion from the New Testament. I hope that much of this will be reasonably straightforward: however, the short studies of the Greek verb *epistrephein* (to turn or to convert) may prove to make greater intellectual demands. But I think my readers will judge that, for the sake of clarity and completion, these sections in the chapters on the Gospels and Acts and Epistles are necessary. Yet it is possible to bypass them, for the general argument of the first part is not dependent upon them: it is merely strengthened by them!

In Part 2 I invite my readers to look at four different approaches to conversion from four eras of the history of the Church. I do this since I fervently believe that we can learn so much from the way in which Christians in earlier centuries have received and understood the Gospel of God concerning Jesus. I realise that looking back for guidance and direction is out of step with the general viewpoints in our culture. Our modern scientists, medical doctors, technologists and cosmologists have little if anything to learn from their predecessors of the last century. Further, we are all used to things becoming out of date or obsolete within a few years. So why should we think that we can benefit from what was believed and done in the fourth or the sixteenth century? The answer is simple. Expertise in spirituality, in knowledge of God and his ways, and holy fellowship with him, may well have been deeper and clearer in earlier centuries than in our own! We certainly look back to Jesus and even farther back to Abraham and Isaiah. We need also to look back to the Church in centuries between the time of Jesus and our own.

I personally find so much encouragement, illumination and insight in the writings of Christians from these periods: I hope my reader will feel it worth while to make the attempt to read and appreciate the examples in Part 2. This will provide a kind of short, selective journey through the history of the Church so that when it is completed we shall be in possession of both a summary of biblical teaching and important examples from the Church's experience of how this teaching has been implemented.

In the light of all this material, I shall invite, indeed urge, my reader in Part 3 to do three things with me: (1) carefully to examine the doctrine of conversion to God which I offer; (2) sympathetically to consider the advice I give concerning the state of convertedness; and (3) passionately to share my hope that the Church in the West will recapture the desire to proclaim the Gospel and to make converts for Jesus Christ.

Finally, the book has three appendixes, two short and one long. The first deals briefly with the subject of conversion in the Old Testament. The second presents an annotated list of verbs from the New Testament which provide the context for talk of conversion. The third is my attempt to present what I find interesting and useful in studies of conversion made by those experts we call the behavioural scientists (anthropologists, psychologists and sociologists).

I truly hope that you will enjoy and benefit from the book as much as I have done in writing and rewriting it. Please read on!

The rest of this chapter sets the somewhat dismal scene in which the churches in Western nations have forgotten, neglected and even set aside their heavenly God-given message of conversion. This has been replaced by a this-worldly secular message. The result has been the decrease of the size and influence of the Church of God in the West.

Setting the scene

Let us be honest. There is little or no enthusiasm for either the concept of conversion or for the effort to win converts for Christ within most congregations of Western Europe and of North America. In fact, conversion is regarded as a taboo subject by some respectable church groups. There are various reasons for this apathy, indifference or even opposition to conversion and we shall turn to some of them below.

First of all, however, it will be helpful to clarify what is meant by such terms as *nominal* and *committed* Christian, and *once-born* and *twice-born* Christian, since these expressions are often used in such a way as to confuse rather than clarify the nature of conversion to God.

A *nominal* Christian is one who is called a Christian because he or she has been baptised (christened) and has some connection with the Church of God. But he is a

Christian in name only: he does not regularly attend divine worship and he makes no special attempt to live as an obedient child of God. In contrast, a *committed* Christian is one who regularly attends Christian worship as a member of a specific congregation and who makes a serious attempt in daily living to serve the Lord Jesus. Such a person would normally be converted, that is turned towards God through the Lord Jesus Christ in faith, hope, love and obedience.

A *once-born* Christian is a person who professes to be a *committed* Christian, but who cannot identify any special moment or period when he or she actually experienced a change of heart and mind towards God. Or, he or she has not had the kind of experience that people who claim to be converted through evangelistic crusades seem to have. Those who can identify a time when they had such an experience of God's grace as to feel that they had been born all over again are the *twice-born*. Of course the *twice-born* ought also to be the *committed* Christian; but this is not universally the case.

What really matters is being in a state of *convertedness*, truly committed to the Lord Jesus Christ: genuine conversion leads to a state of convertedness.

Why apathy?

Now we must return to the theme of indifference to the need for conversion.

(a) Unhappy with crusades

One reason may well be that for many people conversion to God is wholly identified with evangelistic crusades, where it is said that people 'make a decision for Christ' or 'take Jesus into their hearts'. They suspect that in these brisk and bright meetings with the hearty singing and moving testimonies, not to mention the sincere but slick preaching, there is far too much emotional and psychological pressure upon people to go to the front as the preacher presses them to do so. Further, they suspect that those who do claim to have been converted in such a way tend to insist that only the *twice-born* are real Christians: the *once-born* are merely *nominal* because they cannot pinpoint a special moment of 'receiving Jesus'.

There is very obviously a lot of misunderstanding in this whole area and great sensitivity is surely required by those who organise crusades so that in their publicity, preaching and propaganda they do not give wrong or false impressions of how conversion to God must occur. To be fair, we must add that there are those who oppose crusades and evangelistic activity because they are actually opposed to the whole idea of serious, committed Christianity, be it of the *once-born* or *twice-born* variety.

What perhaps we need to recognise is that people go to the front in evangelistic crusades for a variety of reasons. The situation in such meetings is not like that of the apostle Paul preaching to pagans in a Roman city and having to teach not only monotheism (belief in one God) but also the basic facts about Jesus as Lord and Messiah. Most of the people attending crusades are already connected with the Church of God, and the majority of those who go to the front are also connected with the Church. Thus the going to the front can be for such people a determination to become a *committed* rather than remain a *nominal* Christian, or perhaps a fresh dedication of oneself to Christ and his cause. These are but two reasons: often people are not quite clear why they go forward except that they *feel* a need.

Great skill is needed by those who are called the 'counsellors', for unless they perceive why the person has come forward they will give the wrong advice and encourage false understanding. Much more could be said here to reveal the complicated nature of the response made by people to the apparently simple call to 'receive Christ' by coming forward. All, however, that needs to be stated at the moment is that genuine conversions to God-in-Christ do actually occur in these meetings: these are, however, a minority of the genuine 'experiences' of those who make the long walk to the front and then go into the counselling room.

(b) Lack of spiritual confidence

But, leaving aside the use of 'conversion' in evangelistic activity in crusades, we still have to recognise that there is hesitancy and even unwillingness to take conversion, as turning to God-in-Christ, seriously within churches. The underlying reason for this is, I believe, a lack of confidence in God as Saviour and a corresponding lack of confidence in the message of the New Testament as a living Word for today. When a congregation has within it a majority of people who surely know themselves, by God's grace, to be his children and who know that in Christ they are accepted and forgiven, then that congregation will actually talk of the need to make converts and it will take the biblical teaching on turning to God seriously.

Those who know God's joy, peace and love in their hearts also feel a desire to share what they have with others. They hold that, despite all the benefits and privileges that people in Western, affluent society possess, unless they have a right relationship with God in Christ, then their lives are without ultimate meaning and purpose. So they see it as their joyous duty to share what they have received and to seek to make converts. And they do so with a vivid sense that God is the living Lord, and that the message of the New Testament is timely and relevant for people today.

The lack of confidence in God, and the failure to trust in him and rely wholly upon his grace and Word, are caused by a variety of factors. Primarily among these is sin, which is

found in every human heart and which needs forgiveness
and cleansing. But sin affects the whole person and causes
us to turn away from God to seek life, meaning, joy and
commitment only in human activity, means and ends.
Further, when and where there is lack of confidence in God
and his Word, then the institutional churches tend to take
both their agenda and way of operating from what they see
as the 'enlightened' or 'compassionate' thinking and activity
of the society in which they are placed. In practice, this
means that what are usually good things in and of themselves are given priority over what is the best (in terms of
God and his will and Word). The necessity of evangelism
and the need of making converts to God-in-Christ are often
not on the agenda, for it is filled with items of political and
social concern or with items concerned with dialogue with
Marxists and adherents of the religions of the world.

The concern to improve this world and the lot of people
in it is usually undergirded with an 'appropriate theology'.
In recent times this theology has been a theology of the
kingdom of God, which has been seen as God's desire to
have justice operative in this world. Such an interpretation
is right as far as it goes; but what are left out are the whole
dimension of the repentance and faith of the individual and
the supernatural, heavenly dimension of the kingdom as
that which belongs essentially to the age that will come after
the Last Judgment. Let us never forget that an important
ingredient in the Christian message is being saved *from* this
world and from the present evil age!

The concern with dialogue is again a good thing in itself;
but where it has replaced the intention to seek to make
converts then it is being falsely encouraged. Regrettably,
since the doctrine of universalism (the doctrine that all
people, whatever have been their faith and life on earth, will
eventually be 'saved' and enjoy the fullness of eternal life
in the age to come) is assumed as true by many Western
Christians, the 'cutting-edge' of evangelism is removed and

dialogue becomes not an easy but a required and demanding option. There is, of course, no reason why the effort to make converts to God-in-Christ should not itself be accompanied by serious dialogue with those who genuinely want to share what they believe, and to treat others with dignity and respect.

Perhaps the point that I am making will be clearer if I offer an example. As a priest of the Church of England I have attended many deanery and diocesan synods and listened to the debates in the general synod. Further, I have received and read a lot of reports, papers and booklets produced for these synods. The overwhelming feeling I have gained is that of a national Church in retreat, showing as it retreats a genuine concern for the improvement of British society and a desire to 'modernise' itself, in terms of worship and doctrine. In contrast, I have attended several synods of Anglican Churches in the so-called developing or Third World: for example, in Sabah in Malaysia. There I gained a strong feeling of Churches, confident in God and his Word, intending to grow in spiritual power and numbers and to do so without failing to be concerned with the pursuit of peace and justice in this world. They planned for growth!

(c) Lack of heavenly enlightenment

I realise that there are renewed and evangelistically-minded congregations in the traditional, Western churches and I am grateful to God that such exist. But I speak in general of churches which have lost the vision of converting the people of the Western world to the Lord Jesus Christ because they have lost the important grace of heavenly-mindedness. Secularism has so efficiently invaded their theology and practice that enlightenment is seen primarily, or only, in terms of being enlightened about the world in which we live, whose needs are often presented so vividly on the TV screen. Certainly there is talk of the love of Christ and much that is done is laudable (e.g. the practical concern for famine in Ethiopia and the Sudan); but the love of Christ is meant also to send the Church out into the world to make converts and to increase the number of those who, from a renewed heart, genuinely and heartily thank God for his grace and salvation.

As I have referred to salvation, perhaps this introduction is the place to make a brief comment on it in relation to our theme of conversion. It was perhaps easier for the Church in the period before the Enlightenment of the eighteenth century to communicate the need for, and content of, God's salvation in Christ than it is now – especially in our Western society. People then believed in the supernatural and in God and they knew that in many of the problems of life he alone could help them. Conditions in this world were often so bad that it was easy to be convinced that there is life after death and a new and superior order of existence with God. However, the felt sense of helplessness and need did not, of itself, make people the easier to be converted: this is because conversion always includes the recognition of one's own sinfulness and self-centredness and none of us particularly likes such a revelation, even when we are in dire circumstances.

Today there is a widespread conviction that humanity can improve its lot through political, social and economic action; guilt feelings and deep personal problems can be solved by psychiatry and counselling; pain, disease and depression can be relieved or removed by drugs; and scientific and technological developments can solve – perhaps not today but certainly tomorrow – all our problems as they arise. Thus we look for help not from 'outside' our human position but from within it; we believe in a kind of universal salvation through human efforts. And despite much evidence that ought to make us give up this blind faith in human ingenuity, we still tend to believe in it.

Obviously in this situation the temptation presented to the Church is to join in the general way of thinking and offer salvation in the ways of the world, with terms of reference that a this-worldly society can appreciate. And this is what churches in the West have done – at least on the evidence of pronouncements from synods, conferences and councils of churches. And the World Council of Churches (WCC), which would not exist without the financial backing of Western churches, publishes and proclaims many more words on salvation in this world than salvation from sin into the heavenly world to come. Much more is taught about sin as a wrong relationship between people, governments, companies, corporations, nations and races than between human beings and God, their Creator and judge. And much more is said about loving the neighbour (usually on socialist principles) than about loving God with heart, soul, mind and strength. In fact, a careful reading of the publications of the WCC over the last two decades would make one doubt whether, in fact, the member churches actually believed in heaven as the goal of human society, saved by the grace of God in Jesus Christ our Saviour.

Because of this state of affairs, which must trouble all those who believe that God is alive and still offers his eternal salvation freely to all who repent and believe, the Church is becoming of minimal importance in the West and Christianity is being discredited. Unless the Churches recover the vision of the holy God of love who desires that all people receive his salvation and be rescued by his grace from their sinfulness, then the marginalisation of the Church will continue. Unless the Church uncovers and lays bare the basic human predicament – the gone-wrongness of human nature – and then proclaims the salvation of God, calling for people to turn to God, to be converted, to repent and believe the good news concerning Christ, it will become totally ineffectual in a society which will increasingly need to hear a positive, heavenly word.

The truth is that the Church can live only by evangelising and by engaging in mission, to make converts, establish congregations and, as the 'yeast' and the 'salt', change society by the presence of Christ, the light of the world. This book proceeds upon this deeply-held conviction.

PART 1

NEW TESTAMENT
FOUNDATIONS

2

FOLLOWING JESUS

Jesus called upon all who heard him *to believe in the Gospel of God*; and from those who had not been baptised by John the Baptist, he also called for *repentance*. His message was: 'The time has come. The kingdom of God is near. Repent and believe the good news!' (Mark 1:15). John's message had been aimed at turning the Jews towards God in humble expectation of the arrival of God's Messiah (Luke 1:16). Now, Jesus comes on to the scene to announce that the critical moment has arrived: God has begun to act in a new and decisive way to fulfil the promises he gave in centuries past to the prophets of Israel. God is doing something, and will continue to do something which radically affects human beings who are in a state of alienation from, and rebellion against, him. God's anointed one, the Messiah, is now present among the covenant people: through him the sovereign and gracious activity of God in saving and redeeming his people has begun.

In the person of Jesus people are confronted by the gracious, saving reign of God and thus they are challenged to decision – repent and believe the good news of God (as he is present in and acts in Jesus). There are no exceptions – the call is addressed to all Jews of whatever age and rank. Repentance is based on knowledge of God and of his will and is a sincere turning-away from what is not acceptable to him. It is not self-pity and is more than a ceasing to do wrong. Often it includes a sense of shame and sorrow, together with a definite determination of will to repudiate the former life: and it naturally becomes faith in terms of the positive turning towards God for salvation.

In the style of both the prophet and the rabbi, Jesus began his ministry by surrounding himself with a circle of committed disciples. The first of the circle were Galilean fishermen whom Jesus had called to 'follow him' (Mark 1:16–20) by leaving nets and family and learning how to become 'fishers of men'. After a few months Jesus chose from the men who surrounded him twelve to be his special disciples and helpers and to share his mission of proclaiming the kingdom of God (Mark 3:13–19). They actually went out on missions to preach and cast out demons. Probably most of these early disciples or apostles had been disciples of John and saw in Jesus the one of whom John spoke.

The righteous and the sinners

It is not surprising that a general call to conversion should annoy and anger some people. The Gospels provide abundant evidence that those who considered themselves 'righteous' (and were called so by their contemporaries) were particularly offended. In the vocabulary of the Pharisees (those rabbis and scribes who took the keeping of the Law of Moses so seriously and devoutly) the *righteous* man was the one who went to the synagogue at the required times and who sought to keep the Law. In contrast, the *sinner* was the person who did not attend the synagogue regularly and who did not keep the whole Law.

Why should the righteous repent and believe? Did they not already do what God required of them? The Pharisees would not receive the message of Jesus, for it denied much of what they regarded as of supreme importance. Further, the fact that he actually offered God's salvation to the *sinners* (outcasts, tax-collectors, prostitutes and so on) made them wonder whether he was right-minded: for right-minded, righteous people did not eat or have fellowship with the *sinners*. No wonder that Jesus often clashed with the most religious of Jewish people!

Take, for example, the moving incident which occurred at the table during a meal at the house of Simon, a Pharisee (Luke 7:36–50). The host and guests were reclining at table, leaning on one arm and thus exposing their feet and ankles. Without any warning a woman appeared, fell down at the feet of Jesus and began to weep. Then, perhaps embarrassed because she had wet the feet of Jesus, she let down her long hair to use it as a towel to dry his feet: she also kissed them and poured upon them the expensive perfume she had brought to anoint Jesus. Obviously, she wanted to express the deep devotion and love she felt.

The host and local people knew her identity: she was a *sinner*, a local prostitute, and they were offended both by what she had done and also by the fact that Jesus had not rebuked her. So Jesus told the short parable of the two debtors, one who owed a vast amount and the other a small amount. Both debtors had their debts cancelled. So Jesus asked Simon which of them would love the person who cancelled the debt more? The answer was obvious and Simon said the one who had the bigger debt.

Jesus then looked at the woman, her eyes still filled with tears, and said to Simon:

Do you see this woman? I came into your house. You did not give me any water for my feet, but she wet my feet with her tears and wiped them with her hair. You did not give me a kiss, but this woman, from the time I entered has not stopped kissing my feet. You did not put oil on my head, but she has poured

perfume on my feet. Therefore, I tell you, her many sins have
been forgiven – for she loved much. But he who has been
forgiven little loves little.

Jesus was making it clear that her love was a consequence
of the fact that she had repented of her sins and received
forgiveness. Thus he confirmed that forgiveness by publicly
telling her, 'Your sins are forgiven', and followed this by
telling her, 'Your faith has saved you; go in peace.' She was
a repentant, believing and changed woman: having for-
saken her sins she had recognised Jesus as God's Messiah and
felt in her heart the joy of being forgiven. Simon could not
understand because he hardly felt the need for forgiveness.
And Simon, regrettably, is the kind of person not uncommon in our churches.

Jesus met with some success in his ministry to the *sinners*.
We have the records of the conversions of two tax-collectors
who were so despised for their work for the Roman over-
lords that they were excluded from the synagogue and
disqualified from being witnesses in the law-courts.

Take the story of Levi first. He was at the customs post in
Capernaum in the territory of Herod Antipas: he was
probably known to some of the disciples of Jesus who came
from that town. Arriving at the post, Jesus addressed him
forthrightly and authoritatively. In essence he said to him,
'Follow me' (Mark 2:14). No ordinary rabbi gained his
disciples by a command such as this: Jesus's call was com-
parable only to the call to service of the prophets of the Old
Testament (cf. 1 Kings 19:19–21). By this call Jesus established the priority of the divine claim, the reign of God,
above all other claims (of job, family and self). However, it
is a gracious call for it contains the promise of forgiveness
and fellowship.

The kingdom of God dawned as Levi responded to the
call and joyously gave evidence of his new life by making a
feast for Jesus and calling to it all his colleagues and friends in

order that they too could encounter this friend of sinners. If Levi is the one we call Matthew then we know that he became an apostle. No doubt Jesus saw the fellowship at table as an acted parable of the joyous fellowship of the kingdom of God of the age to come, of which this meal in Capernaum was a foretaste. It is not surprising that such a meal caused much local interest, including that of the Pharisees. They were appalled that Jesus should become ritually impure by eating with *sinners*. For them, however, this friend of *sinners* had an ironic word: 'I have not come to call the righteous, but sinners' (Mark 2:17). They needed to realise that they were sinners in the sight of God and only then could they value and pay heed to his call.

Zacchaeus was no ordinary tax-collector: he employed others and then passed on to the Romans what they required. Jericho was a good place for a taxman to be and Zacchaeus had made full use of his position, even though by becoming rich he was despised by the religious leaders. No doubt he had heard stories of Jesus's interest in *sinners* of the kind he was and so he determined to get a good view of him. Being a small man he climbed a tree in order to see over the heads of the crowd. To his great surprise, Jesus stopped beneath the tree and told him to come down for he intended to visit his home. Here again is the forthright and authoritative call to which Zacchaeus felt an urge to respond positively. 'So he came down at once and welcomed him gladly' (Luke 19:6).

We do not know what precisely Jesus said to Zacchaeus in his home, but we do know the result of his explanation of the good news concerning God and his kingdom. Zacchaeus exclaimed: 'Look, Lord! Here and now I give half of my possessions to the poor, and if I have cheated anybody out of anything, I will pay back four times the amount' (v. 8). Repentance here took a very practical turn (as it must have done also with Levi, but Mark gives no details). And Jesus summed up the situation by saying, 'Today salvation has come to this house, because this man, too, is a son of Abraham' (v. 9). The kingdom of God has dawned within the home of Zacchaeus and he was a true son of Abraham, having faith in God of the same kind as the 'father of Israel', Abraham, had.

Before the conversion of Zacchaeus, Jesus made various attempts to bring Pharisees to the point where they would accept him and his message. Luke 15 contains three parables told to Pharisees in order to help them understand why both *sinners* and *righteous* people needed to welcome the dawning of the kingdom of God and enter his gracious, fatherly rule. In the parables of the lost sheep and lost coin Jesus made clear that God is the Lord who seeks, who goes out of his way to rescue sinners and who, with the angelic host, rejoices when he finds one who repents of sin and turns in faith to him. The parable of the lost (prodigal) son is really the story of two sons and provides us with important insights into why both the *righteous* and *sinners* need conversion.

The behaviour of the younger son who squandered his wealth in wild living and who came to feel a great sense of need is easy to understand. The warm and compassionate welcome he received from his father when he returned to the family home illustrates the reception of returning and repenting sinners into the realm of the gracious and fatherly rule of God's sovereign grace.

This festive reception of the prodigal made the elder brother feel bitter: had he not served his father faithfully for a long time but no feast had ever been prepared for him? 'Look!' he said. 'All these years I've been slaving for you and never disobeyed your orders.' Here we see the motivation of the elder brother in his doing of his father's will. He had obeyed not so much as a loving, grateful son, but as a wage-earner. He had distanced himself from his father just as he was distancing himself from his brother. With all his doing of what he was asked to do by his father he had done it without real love in his heart: he had not loved God with all his heart and soul and mind and strength, and he had not loved his neighbour as himself.

Sinners were like sons who had run away from their father and from his commandments: they needed to return in repentance and faith. The *righteous* were like the elder brother, remaining within the sphere of the Law of Moses, but not living as sons of God in a loving relationship with God: they needed to repent of their failure to love God and their neighbour and believe in Jesus, who embodied the compassion and love of God, and be forgiven. For both the *sinner* and the *righteous* a fine welcome was waiting since God, the heavenly Father, through his Messiah, seeks and saves those who are lost. But that welcome was dependent upon the individual – be he *sinner* or *righteous* – saying to heaven: 'God, have mercy on me, a sinner' (Luke 18:13). Here sinner is not a technical term but an existential term describing the state of alienation from God. It is a prayer that every human being ought to pray!

Taking up the cross

Somewhere between the obviously *righteous* and *sinners* were many Jewish people who were, to a lesser or greater degree, pious and faithful. To these, of course, Jesus also proclaimed the good news of the kingdom and of the need to repent and believe. And from time to time he explained what being his disciple and entering the kingdom of God meant. Such an explanation is found in Mark 8:34–8 (cf. Matt. 16:24–8; Luke 9:23–7).

After calling his disciples and the crowd to him, Jesus taught them in these words:

> If anyone would come after me, he must deny himself and take up his cross and follow me. For whoever wants to save his life will lose it, but whoever loses his life for me and for the gospel

will save it. What good is it for a man to gain the whole world, yet forfeit his soul? Or what can a man give in exchange for his soul? If anyone is ashamed of me and my words in this adulterous and sinful generation, the Son of Man will be ashamed of him when he comes in his Father's glory with the holy angels.

Jesus certainly called for decision involving the whole person – feelings (heart), mind and will.

Jesus expected his disciples not merely to disown their sins but also to reject the idolatry of self-centredness. Use of the aorist imperative (*aparnēsasthō* – let him deny [himself]) emphasises that a definite decision has to be taken. 'No' to self: 'Yes' to God. And together with the denial of self, the disciple also has to be ready to face martyrdom – to be ready, for Jesus's sake, to carry the crossbeam of his cross to the place of execution. For if the disciple tries to save his life by denying his master (in, for example, a court), he will thereby lose the gift of eternal life: and, conversely, if the disciple readily loses his life for the sake of Jesus (which is the same as losing it for the kingdom of God), he will gain everlasting life. Once a disciple has forfeited his inheritance of eternal life, there is nothing he can offer to buy it back – not even the whole world. (Probably Jesus had Psalm 49:7–9 in mind as he was giving this teaching, for the thought is very similar.) Further, once a disciple ceases to confess and rejoice in his relationship to Jesus because of his fear of the world, then he cannot expect to be welcomed and owned by Jesus when, as the heavenly Son of Man, he comes to judge the world at the end of the age.

This teaching on personal commitment to Jesus as Messiah was given after he had made it clear that his own path in God's will was via suffering and death, before being vindicated by his heavenly Father (Mark 8:31–3). Therefore, the invitation to follow him was based upon his own commitment to martyrdom if that was the way that the Father ordained. In the history of the early Church the readiness to be a martyr for Jesus's sake was certainly inspired by the example of Jesus himself. Of course, Jesus did not teach that martyrdom was a necessary outcome for all discipleship: what he did teach was the wholehearted nature of commitment to the kingdom of God. In other words, he called for a thorough conversion to God, the God of the kingdom.

Earlier in his ministry, without reference to the possibility of martyrdom, Jesus had clearly emphasised the absolute and prior claims of God upon human beings. When told that his mother and brothers were seeking him, he asked, 'Who are my mother and my brothers?' Then looking at the disciples who had left all to follow him he said, 'Here are my mother and my brothers!' The reason for this seemingly harsh reflection upon his relationship to his family was to make the point: 'Whoever does God's will is my brother and sister and mother' (Mark 3:33–5). In the new family of the kingdom, which Jesus is calling into being, there is required that radical, decisive submission to God, which Jesus himself exemplified in his own obedience to the Father's will. Such submission is the result of conversion – of repentance, faith and baptism.

Sharing the burden

There was an intensely personal touch to the way Jesus proclaimed the kingdom of God. He said: 'Come to me, all you who are weary and burdened, and I will give you rest. Take my yoke upon you and learn from me, for I am gentle and humble in heart, and you will find rest for your souls. For my yoke is easy and my burden is light' (Matt. 11:28–30). His hearers were familiar with the yoke that held together two oxen or asses as they performed some agricultural task.

In contrast to this personal form of address, a typical rabbi would have said something like this: 'Take upon you the yoke of the Law, which God gave to Moses. Your way to God and his salvation is through doing what is commanded in the Law. So receive all the commandments, statutes and ordinances and seek to obey them. It will be burdensome, but you must persevere, and God will help you.' He would have been most sincere, but the yoke he had in mind was the union of the Jew to the Law of Moses, not of the disciple to himself.

Therefore what was unique in the message of Jesus was his insistence that entry into the kingdom of God was through an intimate bond with himself as the Messiah. 'Come to me . . . Take my yoke . . .' and 'learn from me'. To those Jews whose spirits were bent low through the weight of many commandments, Jesus offered relief. He did not set before them an easier way or a less demanding life. He promised to be yoked to each disciple so that he shared the burden, the effort, the striving and the work. Being yoked to Jesus means sharing his vision, going in his way and fighting his cause – and this is the way of the Cross. Conversion is a turning in order to walk with Jesus in his walk with and to God.

The burdens of the average Westerner are certainly moral and spiritual, but they are hardly caused by the weight of the Law of Moses within the conscience. They are caused by the pressures of the secularist society, the consumer society and the technology of the silicon chip. And they are not relieved by more leisure, more alcohol or more luxurious housing. A better or better-paid job may even increase the burdens. These burdens Jesus offers to relieve when a person becomes his disciple, sharing his vision and commitment.

Begotten by God

We find in the well-known parable of the sower (Mark 4:1ff.) some reflection by Jesus upon the response to his proclamation in word, and demonstration in deed, of the kingdom of God. To appreciate this parable we must remember that sowing preceded ploughing in Palestine. This means that the sower is not careless when he scatters the seed everywhere, including the path and where thorns are. It is only in the ploughing and subsequent growth that the nature of the soil is fully revealed. Jesus emphasised the act of sowing, leading to the glorious result of harvest. The main point is not that some seed failed to reach maturity, but that some seed did reach a mature and large harvest. And, in Jewish thought, the harvest was a symbol of the fullness of the glorious kingdom of God.

The fact that not all seed reached maturity, however, allowed Jesus to reflect on the reasons why his message had produced a harvest only in some people. He pointed out that there is the active opposition of evil, spiritual power (Satan, the devil); there is the sinfulness of human hearts, and there is the powerful attraction of this-worldly activities and possessions. Genuine conversion leads to perseverance and commitment, despite all opposition, spiritual and physical.

Therefore, like the prophets before him, Jesus failed to turn the whole nation towards God in repentance, faith and hope. He was very conscious of this and told the parable of the tenants (Mark 12:1–12) who killed the servants (=prophets) and then killed the heir (Jesus, the Messiah). However, he knew that God could not be defeated and that apparent failure and tragedy would be turned to triumph in his vindication through death, resurrection and exaltation.

John, author of the fourth Gospel, reflected deeply on the rejection of Jesus and, in his masterly prologue (1:1–18), provided this explanation of what had happened:

> He was in the world, and though the world was made through him, the world did not recognise him. He came to that which was his own, but his own did not receive him. Yet to all who received him, to those who believed in his name, he gave the

right to become children of God – children born not of natural descent, nor of human decision or a husband's will, but born of God (vv. 10–13).

Jesus is the Incarnate Son of God. He came into the world which he had made and which he sustains. He took to himself the very flesh and human nature which we possess. As Creator he came in his Incarnation to what may be called his own property; further he came to be born a Jew, into the people to whom God had promised the Messiah and in whom God had made preparations to receive him. Tragically those who had been prepared by God's tutelage over the centuries to receive the Messiah rejected him: they were blind and inhospitable. The Jews (in the action of their supreme court, the Sanhedrin) and the Gentiles (in the action of the officials of the Roman Empire) rejected Jesus, condemning him to die as one without rights – the death of a slave.

A minority did, however, receive him as the Messiah: they accepted his claims and readily trusted and obeyed him. Zacchaeus and Levi, along with other disciples, made up this minority. To these believers Jesus, as Incarnate Son, gave the authority or the right to become children of God, united to him in faith and hope and love, and calling him 'Father, dear Father'. Conversion meant that they followed Jesus as children of the heavenly Father.

This minority of Jews became the disciples of Jesus by a definite decision to accept what he said, to turn to God in the way he required, and to follow him wherever he commanded. Each one was conscious of a change of heart, mind and will to become a disciple. This change was a free decision made in response to the authority, the compassion and the challenge of Jesus.

John, however, knew that though conversion to God-in-Christ is a personal commitment involving repentance and faith, it cannot occur without God's direct help. The turning to God and away from sin and self-centredness had to be set in motion by an act of God in and upon the human soul/ will. Therefore he added that those who received Jesus as the Messiah to become the children of God were born (better, begotten) by God. In order to become an infant one has to be begotten by a father and born from a mother. John is stating that the inward, secret, invisible action of God within the human soul which sets off the process of conversion is to be compared with the action of a father's sperm in the creation of a baby. There is no life unless the father first begets and there is no spiritual life as a child of God unless God imparts it.

In teaching the necessity of being begotten by God, John was summarising what Jesus had told Nicodemus, a member of the Jewish Sanhedrin. Their conversation is recorded in John 3. Here are some of the things that Jesus said: 'Unless a man is born from above [begotten from above] he cannot see the kingdom of God'; 'Unless a man is born [begotten] of water and the Spirit, he cannot enter the kingdom of God'; and 'You must be born from above'. The final 'you' is plural for Jesus was addressing Jewry through one of its leaders. Further, if we translate the Greek literally it would read, 'It is indispensable (*dei*) that you (Jews) be born again'. To enter into the kingdom of God and into the new covenant (replacing the Mosaic, old covenant) spiritual life from above was a necessity. And, as the teaching of Jesus in John 3:14ff. makes clear, God gives this new life as people hear the good news and believe on the name of the Lord Jesus. 'God so loved the world that he gave his one and only Son, that whoever believes in him shall not perish but have eternal life' (v. 16).

In the teaching (John 14–16) that he gave to his inner circle just before his crucifixion, Jesus had much to say about the Holy Spirit who would come from heaven as his Paraclete (stand-in, replacement) to take forward the mission of God in the world with and through the disciples. In this discourse, Jesus had this to say about the role of the

Spirit in the conversion of men to God: 'When the Holy Spirit comes, he will convict the world of guilt in regard to sin and righteousness and judgment: in regard to sin, because men do not believe in me; in regard to righteousness, because I am going to the Father where you can see me no longer; and in regard to judgment, because the prince of this world now stands condemned' (16:8–11). Obviously this convicting role of the Spirit is thought of in relation to the proclamation of the good news and teaching concerning the death and vindication of Jesus. They must make clear that all sin is now focused on rejection of Jesus as Messiah and Son; that the only righteousness that is acceptable to God is that of the Son, who is in heaven; and that the devil (Satan) and all his ways and wiles stand condemned by the death and resurrection of Jesus.

After his resurrection but before his final parting, Jesus appeared to his disciples and said: 'All authority in heaven and on earth has been given to me. Therefore go and make disciples of all nations, baptising them in the name of the Father and of the Son and of the Holy Spirit, and teaching them to obey everything I have commanded you. And surely I will be with you always, to the very end of the age' (Matt. 28:19–20). As the reigning Lord in heaven and through the presence of the Holy Spirit as Paraclete, Jesus promised to be with his disciples in their proclamation of himself, making of converts, baptising them and teaching. We shall take up this theme in the next chapter.

In closing this section on the ministry of Jesus, it is perhaps necessary to point out that the message of the necessity of repentance for sin and faith in God through the Messiah does not represent the whole of what is implied in the statement, 'the kingdom of God is near'. In many cases, as the four Gospels show, those who looked to Jesus in faith were healed of diseases and released from demonic possession. The making of people 'whole' was a sign that in the kingdom of God of the age to come there will be no sadness, sickness or death, but joy, wholeness and abundant life.

In the ministry of Jesus this kingdom, like an invading army of liberation, made its presence felt within the conditions of the sinful age. Turning to God in repentance and faith was the response for which Jesus looked, the only response valid before the arrival of the sovereign, gracious and saving rule of God. Likewise, in the mission of the disciples as recorded in the Acts of the Apostles, the kingdom of God was experienced in a variety of supernatural ways through the presence and power of the Holy Spirit, accompanying the proclamation and teaching of the good news of what God had done in and through Jesus, crucified, risen and exalted. In the context of miracles and signs of divine intervention, however, the central call to men remained: 'Repent and believe: turn to God-in-Christ'.

The verb 'to convert'

As you read the Gospels in any of the modern translations, you may be surprised to note that you never seem to meet the verb 'to convert'. Jesus is never said to convert people and people are not said to have been converted. This omission has led some people hastily to conclude that Jesus did not call for conversion, but only for a better kind of living. In fact, we have seen that Jesus made a radical call for repentance and faith, a turning away from sin in order to serve God as a disciple of Jesus. Such a decision and commitment are surely conversion!

However, for the sake of clarity and accuracy, we need to look at the places where the verb 'to convert' can be used and has been used. We shall take the places in the old translation, known as the Authorised Version (King James Version), where the verb is used and place alongside them a modern translation (NIV). Then we shall offer some comments. At this point, as I warned in the Introduction, you will need to make a big effort at concentration!

1. Mark 4:11–12 (Matt. 13:15; cf. John 12:40)

(a) And he [Jesus] said unto them, Unto you it is given to know the mystery of the kingdom of God; but unto them that are without, all *these* things are done in parables: That seeing they may see, and not perceive; and hearing they may hear, and not understand; lest at any time *they should be converted*, and *their* sins should be forgiven them.

(b) He [Jesus] told them, 'The secret of the kingdom of God has been given to you. But to those outside everything is said in parables so that,

> "they may be ever seeing but never perceiving, and ever hearing but never understanding; otherwise *they might turn* and be forgiven!"'

2. Matthew 18:2–3

(a) And Jesus called a little child unto him, and set him in the midst of them, and said, Verily I say unto you, Except *ye be converted*, and become as little children, ye shall not enter into the kingdom of heaven.

(b) He [Jesus] called a little child and had him stand among them. And he said: 'I tell you the truth, *unless you change* and become like little children, you will never enter the kingdom of heaven.'

3. Luke 22:31–2

(a) And the Lord said, Simon, Simon, behold, Satan hath desired *to have* you, that he may sift *you* as wheat: But I have prayed for thee, that thy faith fail not: and when *thou art converted*, strengthen thy brethren.

(b) 'Simon, Simon, Satan has asked to sift you as wheat. But I have prayed for you, Simon, that your faith may not fail. And when *you have turned back*, strengthen your brothers.'

Certainly the translation in the NIV(b) is more accurate than that in the AV(a), which renders the active verb 'turn' by the interpretative passive, 'be converted'. The translators of the AV were so conscious that God is the true cause of all genuine turning to himself that they allowed this theology to influence their translation.

Two related Greek verbs are used: *epistrephein* in Mark 4:12 and Luke 22:32, and *strephein* in Matthew 18:3. Both verbs have the basic meaning of a turning round, be it in the physical or the mental sense (change of mind) or the spiritual sense (turning from sin to God). Examples of the use of these verbs for physical turning or returning occur in Matthew 12:45 and Luke 2:39; for the mental and spiritual sense the verses quoted provide illustrations. We shall encounter further examples in the Acts and Epistles.

Normally these verbs are used intransitively (not having a direct object). However, there is an example in Luke where *epistrephein* is used transitively: An angel of the Lord spoke to Zechariah of the son he would have and said of him: 'Many of the people in Israel *will he bring back* to the Lord, their God' (1:16). In this case the AV translates, '*shall he turn* to the Lord, their God'. We shall encounter a further example of the transitive in James 5:19–20.

Having made general comments it is now appropriate to look at Mark 4:12, Matthew 18:3 and Luke 22:32 in more detail.

The '*they might turn*' of Mark 4:12 refers to those Jews described in Mark 3: they will not believe in Jesus or his message; they actively oppose him and even declare that he is demonic. In this situation Jesus cites Isaiah 6:9–10 as a prophecy being fulfilled in his ministry as it was in that of Isaiah himself. Because of their unbelief, obstinacy and hatred, the Jews cannot appreciate who Jesus is and the nature of the message of the kingdom as he provides it via parables. Thus the Word of God does not enter their hearts and they have no internal conviction that they actually ought to turn to the Lord their God in repentance and faith for his forgiveness and blessing.

The '*unless you change*' of Matthew 18:3 does not refer to a physical change from adulthood to childhood but a turning and changing of the mind so that one's outlook on one's attitude towards life (in particular towards greatness and pride) is altered. Those who would enter the kingdom of heaven/God and thus come under the gracious and fatherly rule of God must repent of pride and self-centredness and humbly submit to the sovereignty of God. The little child embodies the characteristics of trust and humble acceptance as he/she is held by a parent or adult.

Finally, the '*when you have turned back*' of Luke 22:32 refers to restoration after a lapse, and of retracing his steps after going astray in order to return to the right way. Here it is Peter who will face trials and tribulations, but because of the efficacy of the prayer of Jesus he will not lose his faith and will turn back after seemingly losing that faith. We know how Peter denied his Lord and how later, when he heard the cock crow, he wept bitterly. Later he strengthened his fellow disciples. Interestingly, the use of the verb *epistrephein* here is the only occasion in the NT when it is used of the return to God-in-Christ of a disciple who has backslid. Normally, as in Mark 4:12, Matthew 18:3 and other places that we shall note in the Acts and Epistles, it is used of the initial turning to God that is called conversion. Backsliders are usually exhorted to *repent* (e.g. Rev. 2:5, 16, 21f.; 3:3, 19).

Conclusion

There can surely be no doubt that Jesus preached, taught and ministered in such a way as to persuade people that the most important reality they could encounter on earth was the kingly, saving reign of God, the kingdom of heaven. To enter this kingdom as his disciple was for Jesus the supreme human decision while to receive the divine gifts of forgiveness and eternal life was to gain the greatest of all treasures.

Because he was God's agent to bring in this kingdom and to make it permanently available to repentant souls, Jesus gladly submitted to the Father's will. As the chosen servant, he had to become the suffering servant, who having set his face towards Jerusalem was to suffer and die there for the kingdom. But his suffering was not in vain: he suffered as the innocent for the guilty, as the sinless for the sinful. Thus, having paid the debt that sinners owe to God, their judge, Jesus was raised from the dead. Now, in and through him, the Gospel is God's truth for the whole world, and the kingdom is open to all who receive that Gospel. And a person is therefore said to be converted when he receives and obeys the Gospel.

3

TURNING TO THE LORD

We have seen how Jesus proclaimed the kingdom of God as his central message. Yet in the Acts of the Apostles the phrase occurs only seven times and seems to have been displaced by proclamation concerning God's activity in Jesus. The reason for this apparent change in emphasis is that the apostles understood the nature of the kingdom of God in the light of the great redeeming acts of God in the crucifixion, resurrection, ascension of Jesus and of the outpouring of the Holy Spirit. Jesus was now the exalted Messiah, crowned as Lord, and the Holy Spirit, acting in his name, was present in the Church and world. Thus instead of speaking of the kingly, sovereign, gracious reign of God, they spoke specifically of the Lord Jesus Christ, seated at the right hand of the Father, for in him the kingdom of God had its centre and substance.

If we examine the content of the early preaching, recorded in Acts 1–10, we can pick out the essentials of the message of the apostles and evangelists. These were:

1. The prophecies of the Hebrew Scriptures are fulfilled: the new age of salvation is a reality through the coming of Jesus.
2. Jesus was born of the line of King David, as the prophets had foretold.

3. Jesus died sacrificially and vicariously, as the prophets had foretold, in order to deliver us from sin and the present, evil age.
4. Jesus was buried and therefore he was truly dead.
5. Jesus rose victoriously from death on the third day, as the prophets had foretold.
6. Jesus is now exalted to the right hand of the Father as Messiah and Lord and Son, as Psalm 110 had foretold.
7. Jesus will come again to earth as the judge of the world.
8. Forgiveness and acceptance by God are offered to those who repent and believe the good news concerning the Lord Jesus Christ and are baptised.

This, of course, was the message preached to Jews and to those Gentiles or non-Jews who were attached to the Jewish synagogues or were interested in the Jewish faith. The preaching to the pagan Gentiles had to set this basic message in a context appropriate to the understanding and background of the hearers. And, let us not overlook the fact that the preachers proclaimed their message in the power of the Holy Spirit with the definite intention and hope of making converts.

The first conversions

It will be instructive to look at the description of conversion which followed the first evangelistic sermon addressed to Jews by a Spirit-filled apostle. Each year the population of Jerusalem was much expanded at the time of the festivals. At the first Feast of Pentecost (a harvest festival) following the crucifixion, resurrection and ascension of Jesus, the usual large crowds were in the city. Thus, when the waiting disciples of Jesus were marvellously filled with the Holy Spirit, a crowd soon assembled to witness the strange

phenomenon of people seemingly drunk early in the day!
Read Acts 2 carefully to get the details.

Peter took this golden opportunity to proclaim to the
crowd that ancient prophecy was being fulfilled before their
eyes because Jesus, whom the Jewish leaders had caused to
be crucified, is risen from the dead and is the Messiah and
Lord. In fact, as Psalm 110 had predicted, he is at the right
hand of the Father in heaven, and from the Father he has
poured out the Holy Spirit upon his assembled disciples.

Many in the crowd were not only convinced in their
minds as to the truth of Peter's claims but they were also
convicted in their consciences. Since Jesus was the Messiah
their rejection of him had been a sin bringing great guilt
upon their heads. No wonder they cried out, 'Brothers,
what shall we do?' To their surprise, the reply of Peter was
one of great comfort. He did not condemn them but said,
'Repent and be baptised, every one of you, in the name of
Jesus Christ so that your sins may be forgiven. And you will
receive the gift of the Holy Spirit' (Acts 2:38). Being
convicted of sin before God, they are to repent: they are
genuinely to turn away from sin and towards God through
Jesus, the Messiah. Further, they are to submit to baptism in
the name of this same Jesus: that is, to be baptised into his
name as they confess that he is truly the Messiah. And, as
John had promised, as they confessed Jesus as Messiah in
baptism they would receive the gift of the (indwelling)
Spirit from the exalted Messiah.

So we see that what may be called the strands or elements
of conversion are here portrayed as (a) conviction of sin
before God, (b) repentance for sin and turning from it
towards God, (c) belief and trust in Jesus as Messiah, (d)
obedience to Jesus as Lord in submission to baptism, and (e)
(as verses 41–2 make clear) full participation in the life of the
Christian congregation. It is important that we use words
such as 'strands' or 'elements' rather than 'stages' for they
are not to be seen as like a series of steps up which we must

walk. Repentance and faith, for example, are different, but where there is one there is also the other: they cannot be prised apart in experience.

There were about three thousand conversions at the Feast of Pentecost. The Lord added them, as it were, to those who had been disciples of Jesus since before his crucifixion and resurrection. Regrettably we do not have the personal testimony of any single one of this large number of new believers.

What we do have in the Acts of the Apostles is a representative selection made by Luke, its author, of five conversion stories. They deal with people of different background, nationality, temperament and sex. We must now take a look at these and note what they have in common.

Five conversions

1. The Ethiopian (8:26–40)

Philip, the evangelist, who had been preaching in Samaria was sent by God southwards on the Jerusalem–Gaza road. He encountered a covered wagon going southwards and inside was the treasurer of the court of Ethiopia (Nubia rather than Abyssinia). This God-fearing Gentile had been to Jerusalem on a pilgrimage and he was absorbed in the reading of a passage in the prophecy of Isaiah – a part of the Servant Song (Isa. 52:13–53:12). He asked Philip to explain the identity of this servant who 'was led like a lamb to the slaughter'. So Philip was able to explain that this servant of God was the Messiah who entered into God's glory through suffering, death and exaltation. He proceeded to explain the good news of the kingdom of God, revealed and manifested in Jesus, the Messiah.

The Ethiopian was inwardly convinced of the teaching he received from Philip and he had an overwhelming sense of

the need to be baptised, for he saw himself now as a disciple
of Jesus. When they reached the Wadi el-Hesi, north-east of
Gaza, Philip baptised him. And as Philip disappeared the
Ethiopian went on his way rejoicing in the salvation he had
received.

It is possible that in the telling of this story Luke made use
of the narratives of the experiences of Elijah (1 Kgs. 18:12;
2 Kgs. 2:16) and Ezekiel (Ezek. 3:14; 8:3) to describe the
rather miraculous arrival and departure of Philip, as he is
guided and empowered by the Spirit of God.

2. *Saul (9:1–18; 22:1–16; 26:12–18)*

Saul of Tarsus was prominent among those who sought to
stamp out the new movement we call Christianity (8:1–3).
Suitably armed with a commission from the high priest,
Saul left Jerusalem for Damascus, accompanied by an
escort. He intended to purge the synagogues there of the
disciples of Jesus. He had almost reached the walls of that
ancient city when Jesus, the risen and gloried Messiah,
encountered him in an unforgettable vision. About noon a
light shone on and around him, forcing him to the ground
and making him blind. In his ears he heard a voice speaking
in his mother tongue, Aramaic (see 26:14), and saying,
'Saul, Saul, why do you persecute me?' Christ in heaven
was addressing Saul concerning his 'brothers and sisters' on
earth. Bewildered, Saul responded, 'Who are you, Lord?',
to which he got the reply he probably expected, 'I am Jesus
whom you are persecuting.'

We do not know Saul's thoughts as he was taken into the
city where for three days he was not only blind but he took
no food or drink. All we know is that he was visited by a
disciple of Jesus, Ananias, who had been instructed in a
vision to visit him. Ananias laid his hands upon Saul's head,
offered prayer and then witnessed not only Saul's recovery
of his sight but the evidence of his being filled with

(baptised with) the Spirit of the Lord Jesus. Then he said to him: 'The God of our fathers has chosen you to know his will and to see the Righteous One and to hear words from his mouth. You will be his witness to all men of what you have seen and heard. And now what are you waiting for? Get up, be baptised and wash your sins away, calling on his name' (22:14–16). Saul got up, was baptised and took food. He had not only been converted: he had also been filled with the Spirit and given the commission to be an apostle to the Gentiles.

3. Cornelius (10:1–11:18)

Centurions were the backbone of the Roman army: they were non-commissioned officers in charge of a hundred men. Cornelius, a centurion, was much attracted by the monotheism, worship and ethics of Judaism and prayed daily to the God of Israel. He was given a vision in which he was instructed to send men to Joppa and bring back Simon Peter. Meanwhile, the apostle Peter himself also received a vision in which he was given a special revelation in order to persuade him, as a Jew, to consent to visit the home of a Gentile.

Taking six local believers with him, Peter left Joppa with the servants of Cornelius and went to Caesarea where Cornelius showed him excessive homage. In their conversation, to which others eagerly listened, Cornelius recounted his vision and Peter responded by explaining the good news of God's kingdom and of Jesus, the Messiah, who was crucified and now risen. The apostle had not finished his explanatory address when the Holy Spirit fell upon the whole company. The result of this heavenly visitation was that Cornelius and members of his household spoke with tongues, just as the disciples had done in Jerusalem at the Feast of Pentecost after the ascension (Acts 2). The Jewish Christians who had accompanied Peter from

Joppa were amazed and Peter recognised that those upon whom the Spirit had descended and who magnified the Lord Jesus as they spoke in tongues ought to receive baptism for the remission of their sins. So they were baptised in water after they had been baptised by the Holy Spirit.

We must surmise that the hearts of Cornelius and those with him must have been believing the message concerning Jesus Christ even as Peter was giving it to them. They became the first, uncircumcised believers to be baptised and their experience was much discussed in Jerusalem by the elders and apostles. Explaining this amazing event later, Peter actually stated that they did believe in the Lord Jesus Christ and that God had granted them repentance unto life (11:17–18). So though faith and repentance are not clearly portrayed in 10:44–8 (the first account of the conversion of Cornelius) they were present in the experience of those who turned to God-in-Christ. It was, however, the descent of the Spirit followed by such obvious signs that caused Peter, in the light of this divine *fait accompli*, to take the initiative and baptise them.

4. Lydia (16:11–15)

Apparently there was no synagogue in Philippi since there were so few Jewish men there. However, on the Sabbath a number of Jewish women together with a few God-fearing Gentile women met for the traditional service of prayer. Paul and his companions found their meeting-place by the bank of the river Gangites and told them about Jesus, the Messiah, and how he fulfilled the sacred Scriptures by his death, resurrection and exaltation. One lady named Lydia, who was a trader in purple dye, heartily received what Paul explained concerning Jesus and, as a new believer, she (and others of her household) were baptised. Luke comments that 'the Lord opened her heart to respond to Paul's message'. Afterwards she pressed Paul and his companions to be guests in her home. This they did and thus her home became a centre of Christian faith and outreach in Philippi (16:40).

5. *The jailer of Philippi (16:25–34)*

Paul and Silas had been put in prison where they prayed and sang hymns. There was an earthquake which caused widespread damage in the prison, allowing the inmates to escape. When the jailer arrived he made to kill himself – such was the duty of a Roman soldier who had failed. Paul saw him and called him over to where he and Silas were lying injured. He knew who they were and why they were in prison. In the highly charged atmosphere he asked 'Sirs, what must I do to be saved?' Exactly what he understood at this stage about salvation we do not know, but Paul and Silas took this strange opportunity in a shattered prison to recount the good news of Jesus Christ to him and to explain that to receive God's salvation he must believe in the Lord Jesus – trust and obey him. Further, he must share this faith and commitment with his family and household.

After Paul and Silas had explained the Gospel to his household they all expressed their desire to follow Jesus Christ and were immediately baptised – how or where we do not know. Then Paul and Silas were invited into the home for food and fellowship. And as Luke adds, 'the whole family was filled with joy, because they had come to believe in God.'

In looking at all five conversions we can note various common features. In each case there was some form of preparation for conversion. The Ethiopian was a God-fearer who seriously read the Scriptures; Saul was highly trained in the Scriptures and had investigated Christian faith and practice; Cornelius was a God-fearer and a man of prayer; Lydia attended the Jewish meeting for prayer; and the jailer had opportunity of hearing Paul and Silas either before or after their entry into his prison.

Secondly, each heard preaching or teaching about Jesus. Philip explained the Gospel to the Ethiopian; Saul had listened to and interrogated Christians before his vision of the exalted Jesus; Cornelius had a full explanation from Peter concerning God's visitation in Christ; Lydia heard Paul's presentation of the Gospel; and the jailer heard from Paul and Silas the Word of the Lord.

In the third place there is enquiry. The Ethiopian wanted to know the identity of the one described in Isaiah 53; Saul asked the heavenly Jesus to reveal his identity; Cornelius asked the angel in his vision for an explanation of what was happening; and the jailer wanted to know how he could be saved. Only Lydia is not recorded as having made enquiry.

Fourthly, there is evidence of the activity of God. Philip was sent to meet the Ethiopian by direct heavenly command; Saul was given quite unexpectedly a never-to-be-forgotten vision of Jesus and then baptised with the Holy Spirit three days later; Cornelius received a vision and then experienced the descent of the Spirit and speaking in tongues; and the Lord opened the heart of Lydia. Only the jailer is not presented as being the subject of direct heavenly action – unless we see the earthquake in this light.

In the fifth place, each convert is baptised. Only on one occasion (22:16) is the meaning of baptism given: it is for the washing away of sins. It is also entry into the new community, the household of God.

Finally, conversion has immediate results. The Ethiopian and the jailer were filled with joy; Paul felt impelled to preach Christ; Cornelius spoke in tongues and praised God; and Lydia and the jailer offered hospitality.

Regrettably, neither these examples nor indeed the whole contents of the Acts enable us to say with certainty whether genuine conversion to God ought to include that baptism

with the Spirit which Saul and Cornelius received. There
are examples in the Acts of existing believers being filled/
baptised with the Spirit – e.g. the Samaritans (8:5–19) and
Ephesians (18:24–19:7). Because of the prophecy of Joel
(cited by Peter, Acts 2:17–21) and of John the Baptist
(recalled by Jesus, Acts 1:5, and by Peter, Acts 11:16)
concerning baptism with the Spirit and the general evidence
of the Acts, not only modern Charismatics but evangelists
and missionaries of earlier times (e.g. Moody, Finney and
Torrey as well as the late Dr Martyn Lloyd-Jones) have
insisted that the internal work of the Spirit in conversion is
not the same as the 'external' baptism with the Spirit at, or
after, conversion.

The novelty of conversion

The idea of conversion in terms of forsaking one religious
position in order to maintain an exclusive commitment
to another was rare, even absent from the mentality of
the world of the Roman Empire until the arrival of the
Christian evangelists. In *Evangelism in the Early Church* (1970),
Michael Green offers three reasons why the ancient Graeco-
Roman world was not familiar with dynamic, religious
conversion.

First of all, people at that time did not regard belief as
necessary for participation in the cult: you were not required
to believe in the deities that outwardly you worshipped.
Doing what was expected by society in terms of offering
sacrifices and keeping festivals was primary for it had to do
with the supposed well-being of society.

In the second place, people at that time did not connect
morality and ethics with religious observance. Sometimes a
certain ritual purity was required for the period of specific
participation in the cult, but such purity was of short
duration.

And, third, people at that time were not familiar with a
religion that made exclusive claims upon its devotees and
members. To accept Jesus as Lord meant total allegiance
with no other 'Lord' to be obeyed. But to devotees of the
ancient Greek and Roman religions exclusive commitment
was never required.

The spread of Judaism in the Empire, with its fanatical
commitment to monotheism, had caused both admiration
and repugnance. However, Judaism was not a missionary-
minded faith, even though it attracted Gentile converts. The
Christian evangelists called not only upon pagans but also
upon Jews to be converted, to turn to the God who was
revealed in Jesus.

On this novel situation Michael Green comments as
follows:

> It is at this point that the uniqueness of Christian conversion
> stands out. They called on Jews as well as Gentiles to put their
> faith in God's Messiah and join the company of his people. For
> the Gentile this would be conversion *to* a *new* faith; for the Jew it
> would be, in an important sense, conversion *within* the faith in
> which he had been nourished, and of which Christ was the
> summit and goal. But the shock would be as great for the Jew,
> or even greater, than for the Gentile. Both would have to be
> baptised into the Church of the Messiah. And whereas for the
> Gentile that would be much preferable to circumcision, to the
> Jew it was a great stumbling-block. It meant renouncing all
> claim to be God's elect simply on the ground of birth and
> circumcision. It meant becoming like a newborn child, and
> washing away all impurities in the bath of baptism – and that
> was what they were accustomed to thinking took place when a
> proselyte was baptised into Israel. A more humbling renunci-
> ation of all privilege, all acquired and inherited merit and
> standing before God could not be imagined. The *skandalon* of
> conversion to Christianity was absolute (p. 147).

The early preachers saw themselves as witnesses and ambassadors of Christ who in proclaiming the Gospel also saw

the operative power of the Word of God and the Spirit of God. Their absorbing concern was to serve Christ by telling the world of him and calling the hearers to conversion.

The verb 'to convert'

Reading through the Acts of the Apostles, which tells of the expansion of the Church of God through the addition of thousands of first Jewish and then Gentile converts, we find once more that the verb 'to convert' and the noun 'conversion' are not very common! However, we surely agree that the concept and reality of conversion are basic and fundamental to the whole Book.

It is now necessary – again for the sake of accuracy – to do a word study to notice how *epistrephein* and related words are used in the Acts. Our method will be to quote the appropriate verses from the NIV and indicate in italics the word which translates *epistrephein*.

1. 3:19

> Repent, then, and *turn* to God, so that your sins may be wiped out, that times of refreshing may come from the Lord.

The AV translates, 'Repent ye therefore, and be converted', but is alone in using the verb 'to convert'. This call to repentance and turning to God occurs in a sermon delivered by Peter at the gate of the temple in Jerusalem and is addressed to 'Men of Israel'. The turning to God is a turning to God in the sense of believing in and being committed to Jesus as the Messiah. It is a call both to all Jews and to each individual Jew. Earlier Peter had called for repentance by Jews for rejecting and crucifying God's Messiah, Jesus (2:38). There can be no turning to the Lord without repentance.

Peter closed his address to the 'Men of Israel' by speaking of Jesus, who was raised from the dead and who would bless

them 'by *turning* each of you from your wicked ways' (3:26).
Here the verb *apostrephein* is used transitively, and has the
meaning of 'to turn away'.

2. 9:35

> All those who lived in Lydda and Sharon saw him [Aeneas who
> had been healed] and *turned* to the Lord.

All the translations use the verb 'to turn' except the Jerusalem Bible and the New American Bible for Catholics, each
of which have 'were converted to the Lord'. The reason for
the turning/being converted was seeing the miracle of the
curing of Aeneas, a paralytic, by Peter in the name of Jesus
Christ. It is probable that 'all those who lived' means 'a large
number of the residents of' Lydda (OT Lod).

3. 11:21

> The Lord's hand was with them, and a great number of people
> believed and *turned* to the Lord.

Again, only the two RC translations have 'were converted
to the Lord'. The reason for this occurrence of new believers
and converts in Antioch was the testimony for the Gospel
given by Christians who had left Jerusalem for Antioch
during the persecution which led to Stephen's martyrdom.
From this witnessing the Church in Antioch arose.

4. 14:15

> We are bringing you good news, telling you *to turn* from these
> worthless things to the living God, who made heaven and earth
> and sea and everything in them.

Only the NAB uses the verb 'to convert' and translates: 'We
are bringing you the good news that will convert you from
just such follies as these to the living God . . .' Paul and
Barnabas were in Lystra where they healed a man who had
been lame from birth: the local people took them to be gods
appearing as men! Thus Paul appealed to them to listen to

the Gospel concerning Jesus, which called upon them to turn from idolatry to the living God.

5. **15:3**

> The church [in Antioch] sent them [Paul and Barnabas] on their way, and as they travelled through Phoenicia and Samaria, they told how the Gentiles *had been converted*.

Most of the modern versions use the word converted or conversion here. The noun, *epistrophē*, is actually used: therefore a literal translation of the last part of the verse would be, 'telling the conversion of the Gentiles'. It is worthy of note that in verse 4 it is made clear that God is primarily responsible for the conversion of the Gentiles: 'they reported everything that God had done through them'.

6. **15:19**

> It is my judgment, therefore, that we should not make it difficult for the Gentiles who are *turning* to God.

Again only the NAB uses the word 'converts': 'we ought not to cause God's Gentile converts any difficulties'. This is part of James's address at the Council of Jerusalem, where the fact of the conversion of Gentiles had been seriously discussed.

7. **26:17–18**

> I am sending you [Paul] to open their eyes and *turn* them from darkness to light, and from the power of Satan to God, so that they may receive forgiveness of sins and a place among those who are sanctified by faith in me.

Paul is here explaining to King Agrippa how he was called to be an apostle of Jesus to the Gentile nations, and what was the nature of the task before him. In the NIV rendering it is

Paul as the preacher and servant of God who turns them,
whereas in the rendering of the RSV and JB he is to open
their eyes by his preaching and testimony 'that they may
turn from darkness to light'. The Greek has the infinitive,
'to turn', and is used transitively. Behind Paul's words are
those uttered by Isaiah to describe the vocation of the
servant of the Lord in 42:1ff., especially verse 6. The apostle
sees himself continuing the commission of the Servant
(Jesus Christ), to be 'a covenant for the people and a light for
the Gentiles, to open the eyes that are blind, to free captives
from prison and to release from the dungeon those who sit
in darkness' (vv. 6–7).

8. **26:20**

> I [Paul] preached that they should repent and *turn* to God and
> prove their repentance by their deeds.

This is part of the explanation made to Agrippa and describes what was his message to both Jews and Gentiles.

From these texts it is perfectly clear that a message of
repentance and turning/conversion was fundamental for
Peter, James and Paul in their understanding and execution
of their apostleship. Further, as the origins of the Church in
Antioch reveal, the ordinary Christians also saw their calling to include making converts. Turning to God-in-Christ
meant forsaking sin and idolatry and positively turning
towards God in commitment to Jesus Christ as Messiah and
Lord.

Before concluding this brief word study it is necessary to
notice that various words, not related to *epistrephein*, are
translated as 'convert(s)'. In 6:5 and 13:43 *proselytos* (prose-
lyte) is translated as 'Jewish convert' in the NIV and other
versions: in 9:36 *mathetria* (disciple) is translated 'convert' by
the NAB, which also has 'Gentile converts' in 21:25 where
the literal meaning is 'Gentiles who have believed'.

Key words

We have noted how the verb *to turn* has the meaning *to convert*. Further, we have seen that following the proclamation of the good news concerning Jesus and the kingdom of God came the call to the hearers to respond. The response called for was to convert to God in commitment to Jesus Christ. The call was, when given in full, an urging to repentance (turning from sin and evil), to faith/trust (in God and the Lord Jesus Christ) and to baptism (for the forgiveness of sins and incorporation into the new covenant and household of faith). However, we find in the Acts that the response of the hearer is often given in shorthand or in brief.

To obey (*hypakouein*) functions several times as a summary of repent, believe, be baptised. For example in 5:32 the apostle Peter states that God has given the gift of the Holy Spirit 'to those who *obey* him'; and, in 6:7, Luke records that 'a large number of priests became *obedient* to the faith'. The apostle Paul also made use of this way of describing conversion in Romans 1:5 and 6:16, as well as in 2 Thessalonians 1:8. The obedience here described is obedience from the heart, involving emotions, mind and will.

To believe (*pisteuein*) is very common as a synonym for 'to convert'. Disciples of Jesus, the Messiah, are called *believers* (Acts 2:44; 4:32). Not only do they believe in Jesus as God's Messiah, but it is Jesus as the (invisible) exalted Lord. They live by faith and not by sight. Converts are those who *believe in the Lord* (9:42; 10:43; 11:17; 16:31) or simply those who *believe* (13:12; 13:48; 14:1; 17:12; 17:34; 18:8; 18:27; 21:20; 21:25). In all cases it is either stated or assumed that believers are also baptised.

Baptism can be understood at a variety of levels, through various images and as both an act of God and a confession of faith by man. Certainly, becoming a Christian always involved being baptised which was seen as the climax and summary of all that had been going on, both at the human level of repentance and faith and at the divine level of forgiveness, internal spiritual renewal and acceptance into the new covenant and family of God.

Problems of chronology (which comes first, internal rebirth/renewal or faith, and does God forgive the repentant believer before he is baptised?) appear not to have concerned the early Christians: the important point is that they make it abundantly clear that conversion and baptism, baptism and conversion, belong together as the once-and-for-all sacrament of union with Jesus, the exalted Messiah. At a period when those preaching the good news and those receiving it were conscious of the presence and power of the Holy Spirit, there was little or no danger of this sacrament becoming a mere formality or being understood in a magical way. Further, the early Christians accepted the validity and power of ritual and symbol as the very means that the Holy Spirit was pleased to use to effect his work on behalf of the exalted Christ.

4

OBEYING THE GOSPEL

There are twenty-one Epistles of varying length in the New Testament. And there would have been no Christian communities and leaders to which to send these apostolic Letters had not the proclamation of the Gospel, conversions and baptisms occurred! When you read these Letters you have to admit that they were written by men who took the Christian faith absolutely seriously and who fully expected their readers to do the same. So the Letters take the reality of conversion to God as basic, and encourage and exhort the readers to live in such a manner as to adorn the Gospel of God which they have received. Not only are they to live as genuine Christians but also they are to make converts for Jesus.

Obviously we need to be selective in looking at the Epistles. Therefore, since Paul was the acknowledged apostle to the Gentiles, and Peter to the Jews, we shall look at the twin themes of *conversion* and *convertedness* in 1 Peter and Romans. This study will be the more rewarding and meaningful if you have before you the text of these Epistles as you read this chapter. So after opening your Bible, read on.

1 Peter

Any attempt to select material which relates to the event/process of conversion and distinguish it from material

relating to the state of being converted runs the risk
of forcing an arbitrary distinction upon the contents of
an apostolic Letter. This is because the turning to God-
in-Christ in faith and obedience is both a once-for-all
turning and a constant turning and being turned. However,
for our purposes in investigating the concept of conversion, to make use of the distinction is valid – as we shall
see.

(a) The event of conversion

The following relate to the act/event/process of Christian
conversion.

1. Conversion occurs because God *calls* people through
the Gospel of Christ as it is presented in the power of the
Holy Spirit. He is 'the God of all grace, who called you
to his eternal glory in Christ' (5:10; see also 1:15). They
who respond are called the 'elect' (1:1) and the 'chosen'
(2:4).
2. In conversion God sets people aside to serve him. He
does this by 'the *sanctifying work* of the Spirit' (1:2) to make
for himself a special people (2:9) wholly devoted to his
service.
3. God's call is both outward through the Gospel and
inward through the activity of the Spirit. The effect of the
internal activity of the Spirit is likened to a *new birth* – an
entrance into eternal life and a new relationship and communion with God. 'In his great mercy he [God] has given
us *new birth* into a living hope' (1:3) so that 'you have been
born again, not of perishable seed, but of imperishable,
through the living and enduring word of God' (1:23). The
internal action of the Spirit is, as it were, parallel to the
outward hearing and receiving of the dynamic truth of the
Gospel.

4. To be a convert means to be a *believer* in the Gospel of God concerning Jesus Christ whom he raised from the dead. 'Through him [Christ] you *believed* in God, who raised him from the dead and glorified him, and so your faith and hope are in God' (1:21). Christians are those who '*believe* the word' (3:1).

5. A believer is also one who *obeyed* the call of the Gospel. Then 'you have purified yourselves by *obeying the truth*' (1:22) to enter into a life of *obedience* to Jesus Christ (1:2).

6. To believe and to obey is also to *come* to God-in-Christ and to *taste* that the Lord is truly good (2:3–4).

7. To believe, to obey and to come is to be *won over* to the cause of Jesus Christ (3:1). Wives with pagan husbands ought to be so pure in living that through their influence their husbands may be won over from idolatry and impurity to the Christian way (3:1ff).

8. Conversion is from a life of idolatry and unrighteousness. 'For you have spent enough time in the past doing what pagans choose to do – living in debauchery, lust, drunkenness, orgies, carousing and detestable idolatry' (4:3). It is also from a life characterised by darkness (2:9) and ignorance (1:14).

9. Conversion is becoming a sheep in the flock of Christ the Shepherd. 'For you were like sheep going astray, but now *you have returned* to the Shepherd and Overseer of your souls' (2:25).

10. The climax of conversion is in *baptism*, which is an effective sign of what God is doing within and for the believer. 'Baptism now saves you also – not the removal of dirt from the body but the pledge of a good conscience towards God. It saves you by the resurrection of Jesus Christ ...' (3:21). The pledge of a good conscience probably refers to the satisfactory confession of personal faith made at the baptism, which is the symbol and sacrament of dying to sin and rising to new life in and with Christ.

Conversion is a rich concept, pointing to the total move from idolatry, through obedience to the call of God in the Gospel and trust in Jesus Christ, to baptism and membership of the community of those who are set aside for the service and worship of the living God.

(b) Convertedness

The following may be said to relate to the state of being turned to the Lord.

1. Being turned towards God makes the believer a *stranger* in this world (1:1) because his true home is with Christ in the heavenly realm. Christians are to live their lives as strangers here in reverent fear of God.

2. Being turned towards God makes the believer *a member of the people of God*. 'But you are a chosen people, a royal priesthood, a holy nation, a people belonging to God, that you may declare the praises of him who called you out of darkness into his wonderful light' (2:9). The new people of God exist to glorify God and to enjoy him for ever.

3. Within the people of God, each person is to be *built up in genuine faith, hope and love* (2:4–5).

4. Being turned towards God implies and requires *a life characterised by love and compassion*. There is the loving of Christ himself (1:8), and the loving of the community of believers (3:8). 'Above all love each other deeply, because love covers over a multitude of sins' (4:8).

5. Christian life is *filled with joy*, even when there is suffering to endure for Christ's sake. 'Though you do not see him [Christ] now, you believe in him and are filled with an inexpressible and glorious joy, for you are receiving the goal of your faith, the salvation of your souls' (1:8–9). And,

'rejoice that you participate in the sufferings of Christ, so that you may be overjoyed when his glory is revealed' (4:13).

6. Being turned towards God means *glad submission to Jesus as the Master.* 'But in your hearts set apart Christ as Lord' (3:15).

7. Being turned towards God implies *a readiness to witness to his grace.* 'Always be prepared to give an answer to everyone who asks you to give the reason for the hope that you have. But do this with gentleness and respect . . .' (3:15–16).

8. Being turned towards God implies *a life conformed to his will and characterised by purity and reverence.* 'As obedient children, do not conform to the evil desires you had when you lived in ignorance. But just as he who called you is holy, so be holy in all you do . . .' (1:14–15). And true beauty is 'the unfading beauty of a gentle and quiet spirit, which is of great worth in God's sight' (3:4).

9. Being turned towards God implies *a desire to know more about him and enjoy a deeper communion with him.* 'Like newborn babies, crave pure spiritual milk, so that by it you may grow up in your salvation . . .' (2:2).

10. Being turned towards God involves *a pilgrimage towards the kingdom of God of the age to come, a pilgrimage characterised by hope.* 'Praise be to the God and Father of our Lord Jesus Christ! In his great mercy he has given us new birth into a living hope through the resurrection of Jesus Christ from the dead, and into an inheritance that can never perish, spoil or fade – kept in heaven for you . . .' (1:3–4).

Convertedness is also a rich concept, highlighting life within a new community which sees itself as belonging first and foremost to Jesus Christ and thus living in faith, hope and love. This community belongs to the heavenly realm where Christ is and so it is never wholly at home in this world. Yet, while in this world, it exists to glorify God and

to increase through conversions the number of those who
live to praise the Lord.

Romans

Paul's Epistle to the Romans is rich in theological concepts
and is the kind of Letter that can be studied over and over
again, each time bringing new insights. Therefore any brief
summary offered here will of necessity only, as it were,
scratch the surface.

(a) The event of conversion

1. Turning to God is *a response to the call of God*, made by the
preacher of the Gospel and in the power of the Spirit. Paul
and other apostles were 'to call people from among all the
Gentiles to the obedience that comes from faith' (1:5); and
through the human call God himself called them 'to belong
to Jesus Christ' (1:6) and 'to be saints' (1:7); this call is an
effectual call for 'those he predestined, he also called; those
he called, he also justified' (8:30).
2. At the heart of turning to God is *faith* – believing the
Gospel. 'I am not ashamed of the gospel, because it is the
power of God for the salvation of everyone who believes'
(1:16). The Gospel is the power of God unto everlasting
salvation because it sets forth God's gift of righteousness to
those who believe. Thus 'the righteous will live by faith'
(1:17).
3. What God gives in conversion is the *gift of righteousness*. As
the sinner believes, he is placed in a right relationship with
God because the guilt of his sin is cancelled and he is viewed
by God as being clothed with the perfect righteousness of
Christ. 'This righteousness from God comes through faith
in Jesus Christ to all who believe' (3:22). And faith in Christ

is faith in the living Lord who died to make atonement for sin and rose in order to bring the gift of righteousness to believers (3:22ff.; 4:25).

4. Turning to God occurs as there is a *turning away from godlessness and wickedness, idolatry and unrighteousness* (1:18ff.). Conversion is ceasing to be a slave of sin and becoming a slave of God and of righteousness (6:22).

5. Turning to God occurs as there is a *turning away from attempts to gain salvation through keeping the Law of Moses.* Because of the sin within the human heart, no person can keep the Law of God perfectly and with the right motives: to the sincere person the Law becomes the means of making him aware of how sinful he is (7:7ff.). This is why salvation is by faith leading to faithfulness as a dutiful and loving slave of God.

6. At the centre of the experience of conversion is *the confession, 'Jesus is Lord'* – 'for it is with your heart that you believe and are justified, and it is with your mouth that you confess and are saved' (10:10). For Paul to call Jesus 'the Lord' was absolutely fundamental for the truth of the Christian faith. This was the title that above all titles revealed the identity and saving work of Jesus, the Son of God. The confession, 'Jesus is Lord' was formally made at baptism.

7. *Baptism is the climax and sign* of conversion. This is because baptism symbolises union with Christ, incorporation into his death and his resurrection. 'Now if we died with Christ, we believe that we will also live with him' (6:8). And union with Christ means membership of his body, the Church (12:4ff.).

Conversion relates to the move from a life of sin in Judaism or paganism through responding to the call of God in the Gospel and through baptism to membership in the body of Christ. It is the beginning of a life of faith and of a right relationship with God. Justification by faith is being placed

by God in a harmonious and right relationship with himself
as one trusts in Jesus as Lord.

(b) Convertedness

1. To be turned towards God is to be *at peace with God*. 'Therefore since we have been justified through faith, we have peace
with God through our Lord Jesus Christ, through whom
we have gained access by faith into this grace in which we
now stand' (5:1–2). Because believers are reconciled to God
they can enjoy intimate spiritual communion with him.

2. To be turned towards God in Christ is *to enjoy the internal
presence and power of the Holy Spirit*. Paul has much to say about
this theme, especially in Chapter 8. The presence of the Spirit
means that life can be lived not at the level of following the
natural, fleshly desires and passions, but at the level of the
will of God. Further, his presence means that the love of
God is released in the human heart (5:5), that he brings the
conviction and humble confidence that one is truly a forgiven and blessed child of God (8:15) and that he assists not
only in prayer (8:23) but in all the difficulties of life (8:26).

3. To be turned towards God in Christ is *to rejoice in hope of the
glory of God*. 'And we rejoice in hope of the glory of God' (5:2)
and we 'consider that our present sufferings are not worth
comparing with the glory that will be revealed in us' (8:18).
There is joy because God is on our side and if he is on our side
who can be against us (8:31ff.)? There is fullness of life with
him and for him in the glorious kingdom of the age to come.

4. To be converted means *living as a slave of God and of his
righteousness*. There is a responsibility placed upon all
Christians actively to offer their whole persons to God for
his service (6:19ff.). 'I urge you, brothers, in view of God's
mercy, to offer your bodies as living sacrifices, holy and
pleasing to God – which is your spiritual worship' (12:1).

5. To be converted means *fully participating in the life of the
people of God*. 'Just as each of us has one body with many

members, and those members do not all have the same function, so in Christ we who are many form one body, and each member belongs to all the others' (12:4–5). And, 'Each of us should please his neighbour for his good, to build him up' (15:2).

6. To be converted means *being concerned about the conversion to God-in-Christ of both Jews and Gentiles*. Paul expressed his fervent hope for the future conversion of the whole Jewish people (11:25ff.) and asked for the help of the Roman Church in his mission to the Gentiles (15:14–33). This concern will express itself in various forms of witness, service and prayer. Paul's last words in the Letter to Rome are his prayer that 'all nations might believe and obey him [the eternal God]' (16:26).

7. To be converted requires *living in such a manner that you are prepared at all times to meet Christ if he should come as judge*. 'The hour has come for you to wake up from your slumber, because our salvation is nearer now than when we first believed. The night is almost over; the day is almost here. So let us put aside the deeds of darkness and put on the armour of light . . . clothe yourselves with the Lord Jesus Christ, and do not think about how to gratify the desires of the sinful nature' (13:11–14).

Perhaps Paul's richest teaching concerning the life of converts is in Chapter 8 where he describes and delineates what being indwelt, empowered and guided by the Holy Spirit (who is the Spirit of Christ) really means. This life stands in such contrast to the life lived only in the strength and insights of human nature (however cultured and trained that nature is). Then also Paul was insistent that those who are justified by faith are also those who 'count themselves dead to sin but alive to God in Christ Jesus' and so do not 'let sin reign' in their mortal bodies (6:11–12). Baptism is the sign, seal and symbol of a radically different life of divine quality.

Whether we begin with the theology of Peter or that of Paul
what is very impressive and rather overwhelming concerning conversion is (a) the cost to God himself of making
conversion possible for sinful human beings, and (b) the
nature of the claims made concerning the convert's relationship with God, his Creator and judge. The whole teaching
concerning conversion places it within the realm of the
supernatural.

The cost to God is presented in terms of the Incarnation of
the eternal Son – an Incarnation that involved not merely
taking to himself a human nature and human flesh, but also
in that humanity suffering as the innocent one on behalf of
the guilty and bearing the wrath of God which he did not
deserve. And he suffered, died and was buried for the
salvation of those human beings to whom he was united
through possessing that human nature they possessed.

The benefits and blessings of conversion belong more to
the realm of the supernatural and eternal than to the natural
and finite, although they do effectively impinge upon and
into the latter. In conversion the believing sinner both enters
into a new, everlasting relationship and communion of love
with God, whom he now knows as 'Abba' (Daddy) and also
is given the indwelling presence of the Holy Spirit. In union
with Christ he belongs to that heavenly realm where Christ
is exalted as Lord and as such he is a pilgrim and sojourner
on earth.

Yet the Christian community is called to live on earth in
imitation of Christ, witnessing to his love and power, his
holiness and compassion. For believers to be what by
conversion they ought to be requires their wholehearted co-
operation with God's will and grace as well as their complete commitment and dedication as disciples of Jesus the
Lord. And it is in this area that problems arise, as the
individual Christian and the Christian fellowship/society
fail to live up to the high calling of God in Christ Jesus. It is
not surprising, bearing in mind what human nature is like,

that the New Testament contains many exhortations to disciples and believers to make every effort to receive and utilise the help and grace of God, available to assist them live as they ought to live.

And now, to close this chapter, we need for the sake of accuracy and completion, to note where and how the verb *epistrephein* is used in the Epistles of the New Testament.

The verb 'to convert'

Our method will again be to use the NIV and to indicate in italics the translation of *epistrephein*.

1. 2 Cor. 3:16

But whenever anyone *turns* to the Lord, the veil is taken away.

Here Paul is referring to people who live under the terms of the old covenant. It is as though a veil covers their eyes and dulls their minds and they cannot see the glory of God in the face of Jesus Christ. This impediment is removed as they respond to the Gospel concerning the Lord Jesus. Paul has in mind the example of Moses who 'whenever he entered the LORD's presence to speak with him, he removed the veil until he came out' (Exod. 34:34). He also has in mind the fact that this turning to the Lord which removes the veil of ignorance and sin is achieved through the invisible assistance of the Spirit of Christ (2 Cor. 3:17).

2. Gal. 4:9

But now that you know God – or rather are known by God – how is it that *you are turning back* to those weak and miserable principles? Do you wish to be enslaved by them all over again?

Here Paul is talking about converting back to the superstitions and idolatry from which the church members in Galatia had originally turned as they converted to God-in-Christ. Indeed so worried was Paul by the possibility of their

backsliding under pressure from false teachers (Judaisers)
that he wrote: 'I fear for you, that somehow I have wasted
my efforts on you' (v. 11). Though Paul had a very high
sense of the faithfulness of God in keeping his children
within his salvation, he did nevertheless repeatedly warn of
the possibility of converting back to the old life and religion.

3. 1 Thess. 1:9–10

> . . . you *turned* to God from idols to serve the living and true God,
> and to wait for his Son from heaven . . .

Here Paul described the conversion of the Thessalonians to
God. They converted from idolatry to serve the one, true
deity and to live in hope of the second coming of the Lord
Jesus Christ from heaven. In a society where polytheism
and idolatry were an important part of the culture, the
moving away from these into commitment to the one, true
and living God was a major step with consequences of many
kinds. And the expectancy, or the 'watching and praying'
involved in this commitment added a definite element of
hope, so that the converts both look up to the exalted Christ
and look forward in time for his coming.

4. Jas. 5:19–20

> My brothers, if one of you should wander from the truth and
> someone should *bring* him *back*, remember this: Whoever *turns* a
> sinner from the error of his way will save him from death and
> cover a multitude of sins.

James sees the Church as a redemptive brotherhood
through whose efforts the wandering or erring brother can
be restored, being turned back to righteousness. In these
verses we encounter the verb *epistrephein* being used in the
transitive sense, recalling Luke 1:16–17 where John the
Baptist is presented as he who will turn many of the sons of
Israel to the Lord their God.

5. 1 Pet. 2:25

For you were like sheep going astray, but now you have *returned* to the Shepherd and Overseer of your souls.

Sheep without a shepherd wander aimlessly but with their shepherd go towards suitable pasture and safety. The church members to whom Peter wrote had also been lost without a Saviour and master but having turned to God they have found their shepherd, who is their pastor. This thought of converts being like returning sheep is taken from the description of the role of the suffering servant in Isaiah 52:13–53:12.

6. 2 Pet. 2:21–2

It would have been better for them not to have known the way of righteousness, than to have known it and then *to turn* their backs on the sacred commandment that was passed on to them. Of them the proverbs are true: 'A dog *returns* to its vomit,' and 'A sow that is washed goes back to her wallowing in the mud.'

Peter is referring to people who have known the way of righteousness (Christianity) and escaped from the world's defilements. He is therefore talking about apostasy, a turning from the 'sacred commandment' by which Peter means the oral tradition of Christian teaching. The second occurrence of 'turn' in the proverb has no theological meaning, just as there is no theological meaning in the 'I turned' of Revelation 1:12.

To these occurrences of *epistrephein* we may add the places where the related verb *apostrephein* is used. In Romans 11:26 we find the transitive sense as the Messiah is said to turn godlessness away from Jacob; in 2 Timothy 4:4 and Titus 1:14 people are said to turn from the truth and reject it, while in Hebrews 12:25 there is warning to believers not to turn away from God. The use in 2 Timothy 1:15 is physical desertion of Paul by colleagues.

The total message of all these occurrences of turning or being turned is that even as there is a definite turning to God from sin, idolatry and superstition so there is also the ever-present possibility of a returning in the direction from which the convert originally came. (The possibility of full apostasy seems to be indicated in the New Testament – see 1 Cor. 10:1–12; Heb. 3:12–18; 6:6; 10:26, 38f.; and Jude 4–6.) While the turning to God is only possible through the help of the Holy Spirit, the returning to the old life is possible through the definite rejection of the help of the Spirit and the teaching once received and known.

This teaching stands as a permanent warning to converts to Jesus Christ. Regrettably, it would be possible to write a book of examples of people who, having claimed to be Christians and showed signs of new life, later fell away and disowned the Lord Jesus.

Conclusion

Our study of the New Testament is now completed – except for Appendix 2, to which you may like to turn now.

Before moving on to Part 2, it will be beneficial to remind ourselves of what we have learned concerning conversion. First of all, we have seen that it cannot happen without the direct (yet invisible) action of God (a) giving power to the word of the Gospel received through ear and eye in the mind, and (b) preparing the heart, mind and will to receive the Gospel positively, and to obey it joyfully. Then, in the second place, he or she who reads/hears the Gospel is aware of his/her need of God's grace, to repent of sin, to believe and trust in the Lord Jesus, and to submit to him as Lord in the fellowship of his Church. We have called this human response the strands or elements of conversion.

We have become aware that the action of God and

response of the human being to the Gospel cannot be fitted into any specific method or timescale. Converted people are not like identical cars that come from the production line. They are more like a multitude of different paintings produced by one great artist: all have a likeness but all are different. Bearing this in mind, we prefer this definition of conversion: *In response to the Gospel, a person turns to God, who is Father, Son and Holy Spirit, in repentance and faith, in order to trust, love, worship and serve him as a member of his Church.*

In Part 2 we shall take four examples from the long history of the Church to reveal how the event of conversion has been understood and managed by the Church in different periods and places. We could offer further examples, but these four will serve to show the variety of approach to conversion that God, in his mercy, has been pleased to use to extend the size of his Church.

PART 2

MODELS OF CONVERSION

5

THE CATECHUMENATE MODEL

In the first five or so centuries of the Church, people inside and outside the Roman Empire were attracted to Christ and Christianity by a variety of factors – e.g. the intellectual and moral appeal of the faith, the example of the martyrs, acts of compassion by Christians and the vitality and holiness of the congregations. Whatever were the external means that set in motion the response to the Gospel and the turning to God, each individual seeker after God-in-Christ normally had to become a catechumen. This involved receiving instruction in the faith, being examined and then being baptised and received into full membership, usually at the Easter festival. The climax and fulfilment of conversion was the sacrament of baptism, understood as *God's sign and symbol*, in and through which he poured out his grace and his Spirit upon the believing, confessing sinner.

With our modern interest in the journey into faith, we today would like to read testimonies from individuals of their experience before entering the catechumenate. These would tell how the slave or patrician lady first learned of Christ, desired God's salvation in Jesus and was prepared for persecution in forsaking idolatry to join the Church. Regrettably such testimonies are very rare because they were not written down and preserved. However, we do possess the testimony of Cyprian as to the high view of baptism as the sacrament of conversion, and the testimony of Augustine as to how he came to submit to Jesus Christ and desire baptism. We must now look at these.

Two testimonies

Cyprian (d. 258) was a rich, cultured Latin-speaking North African, who was a pagan orator (rhetorician). In the year 246 he was converted to Jesus Christ. Writing to Donatus he explained what had happened at his baptism in these words:

> I was myself so entangled and constrained by the very many errors of my former life that I could not believe it possible for me to escape from them, so much was I subservient to the faults which clung to me; and in despair of improvement I cherished these evils of mine as if they had been my dearest possessions. But when the stain of my earlier life had been washed away by the help of the water of birth, and light from above had poured down upon my heart, now cleansed and purified; when I had drunk the Spirit from heaven, and the second birth had restored me so as to make me a new man; then straightaway in a marvellous manner doubts began to be resolved, closed doors to open, dark places to grow light; what before had seemed difficult was now easy, what I had thought impossible was now capable of accomplishment; so that I could now see that what had been born after the flesh and lived at the mercy of sin belonged to the earth, while that which the Holy Spirit was enlivening had begun to belong to God.

Cyprian became the Bishop of Carthage and a distinguished Christian leader.

Augustine (354–430) was also born in North Africa and became a bishop there – at Hippo. His conversion occurred in Milan in 386. He was a professor in the city and knew of the Christian faith through his mother, Monica, as well as through the preaching of the famous Ambrose, Bishop of Milan. The decisive event occurred when he was with his companion, Alypius, in the garden of the lodging where they lived.

A strong surge of thought dredged from my secret depths and cast up all my misery in a heap before my inner eye. A mighty tempest arose bearing a great storm of tears. To shed it with befitting speech, for to be alone seemed the better state for weeping, I rose from Alypius' side, and withdrew some distance, so that even his presence should not be an embarrassment to me. Thus I thought, and he was sensitive. I think I had earlier said something in which the sound of my voice made it clear that I was heavy with tears. I thus arose, while he stayed where we had been sitting, greatly amazed. I flung myself carelessly down under some fig tree, and let the reins of weeping go. The streams of my eyes broke forth, a sacrifice acceptable to you. I said to you, in words something like these: 'And you, O Lord, how long, how long? Will you be angry for ever? Remember not past iniquities.' For I felt I was in their grip and I cried out in lamentation: 'How long, how long, tomorrow and tomorrow? Why not now? Why not an end to my vileness in this hour?'

Such were my words and I wept in the bitter contrition of my heart. And, see, I heard a voice from a neighbouring house chanting repeatedly, whether a boy's or a girl's voice I do not know: 'Pick it up and read it, pick it up and read it'. My countenance changed, and with the utmost concentration I began to wonder whether there was any sort of game in which children commonly used such a chant, but I could not remember having heard one anywhere. Restraining a rush of tears, I got up, concluding that I was bidden of heaven to open the book and read the first chapter I should come upon. I had heard of Antonius that from a public reading of the gospel he had chanced upon, he had been commanded as if what was read was said especially to him: 'Go, sell all that which you have, give it to the poor, and you shall have treasure in heaven, and come and follow me', and that by such a word from God, he had been immediately converted to you. Excitedly then I went back to the place where Alypius was sitting, for there I had put down the apostle's book when I got up. I seized it, opened it and immediately read in silence the paragraph on which my eyes first fell: '. . . not in the ways of banqueting and drunkenness, in immoral living and sensualities, passion and rivalry, but clothe yourself in the Lord Jesus Christ, and make no plans to glut the body's lusts . . .' I did not want to read on. There was no need. Instantly at the end of this sentence, as if a light of confidence had been poured into my heart, all the darkness of my doubt fled away.

Putting my finger or some other mark in the page, I shut the book and with a calm face now I told Alypius, and he thus made known to me what had taken place in his heart unknown to me. He asked to see what I had read. I showed him. He read on, and I did not know what followed. It was this: 'Let the weak in faith receive.' He took it to himself and showed it to me, and by such admonition he was given strength, and to that resolution and purpose without any stormy hesitation he applied himself along with me. This was most like him, for his was a character which had long been much, much better than mine. Then we went inside to my mother, and told her to her joy. We told her the course of events. She rejoiced triumphantly, and blessed your name, 'who are able to do above all that we ask or think.' She saw that you had given her so much more concerning me than she had sought with her pitiful and tearful lamentations. You converted me to yourself, so that I no longer sought a wife nor any hope in this world, standing on that rule of faith in which so many years before you had shown me to her. You change her grief to joy, more richly than she had desired of you, and a joy more cherished and chaster than she sought from grandchildren of my body.

Later in the *Confessions* Augustine tells of his preparation for baptism and of being baptised by Ambrose, along with Alypius. He saw this event as the means used by God to forgive his sins and to bring him new, spiritual birth. Thus he states that with his friend he was baptised and 'anxiety over our former living fled'.

The catechumenate

By the third century, in each of the larger churches there was a catechetical class/school of those who had been accepted as candidates for holy baptism. Here they were taught not only the doctrinal content of the faith but were also instructed in morality and spirituality – e.g. how to pray. Each Sunday all the catechumens were expected to attend the Eucharist, but they only stayed for the first part, the ministry of the Word and of prayer, being excluded from the Holy Communion. The latter was seen as the sacrament only for the baptised, faithful membership.

The admission of a person into the catechumenate required that she/he have as a guarantor a member of the congregation and that her/his reasons were honourable. Slaves had to get the permission of their masters and those with certain occupations (e.g. pagan priest, astrologer, actor and charioteer in the circus) had to relinquish them. Strict rules governed sexuality and candidates with irregular relationships were required to put them right. At the actual admission each candidate was given the sign of the Cross and she/he was considered as a newly-conceived foetus growing within the womb of holy, mother Church towards birth in holy baptism. The period of instruction lasted anything from several months to three years and ended with a solemn examination, conducted by the bishop a few weeks before Easter.

Final preparations for baptism occurred in holy week and included acts of penance, renunciation of Satan, exorcism, the bishop's teaching concerning baptism and membership of the Church, and one or more nights of prayer and fasting (certainly on the Saturday night before Easter Day). The catechumenate ended at daybreak on the Sunday when the rite of baptism began.

So much, of course, depended upon the quality of the teachers (who were either ordained or lay) and the leadership of the local bishop in terms of the preparation for baptism and understanding of union with Christ and membership of the Church. There is quite a large amount of material extant from the fourth and fifth centuries which represents the teaching given by bishops to their candidates in the week before baptism. Recently Raymond Burnish has published a study of the teaching given in Jerusalem, Antioch and Mopsuestia by the bishops, Cyril, John Chrysostom and Theodore, in his book *The Meaning of Baptism*. This book is worth reading if for no other reason than to see just how highly the sacrament of baptism was regarded. For example, John Chrysostom told his candidates in Antioch the following concerning the bath of regeneration into which they were soon to be plunged.

> This bath does not merely cleanse the vessel but melts the whole thing down again. Even if a vessel has been wiped off and carefully cleansed, it still has the marks of what it is and still bears the traces of the stain. But when it is thrown into the smelting furnace and is renewed by the flames, it puts aside all dross and, when it comes from the furnace, it gives forth the same sheen as newly-moulded vessels. When a man takes and melts down a gold statue which has become filthy with the filth of years and smoke and dirt and rust, he returns it to us all-clean and shining. So, too, God takes this nature of ours when it is rusted with the rust of sin, when our faults have covered it with abundant soot, and when it has destroyed the beauty he put into it in the beginning, and he smelts it anew. He plunges it into the waters as into the smelting furnace and lets the grace of the Spirit fall on it instead of the flames. He then brings us forth from the furnace, renewed like newly-moulded vessels, to rival the rays of the sun with our brightness. He has broken the old man to pieces but has produced a new man who shines brighter than the old.

We must remember that this is sermonic material and is designed to make an important point for ordinary people: that in baptism, conversion to God reaches its climax and after baptism the one baptised is a new person and is to live as such.

Earlier we noted that the elements or strands of genuine conversion were conviction of sin, repentance, faith in

Jesus, baptism and incorporation into the living Church. Now we may observe that, where the catechumenate was operating well, these strands had an excellent chance not only of being genuinely present but of being bound together within the experience of the catechumen, sealed as it were by the knot of baptism.

A baptismal liturgy

Though it would be possible to provide an example of the kind of baptismal service used by John Chrysostom, we do possess a text from much earlier. In the *Apostolic Tradition* of Hippolytus from around 215 we have a service which professes to be an account of the liturgical and pastoral practices then current in the Church in the city of Rome. Here is how the final preparation for baptism and the baptism itself are described. It seems that while the majority baptised were adults there was the occasional child from a Christian home.

First of all here are the instructions for the final preparation of candidates for baptism. They include testing for genuine repentance.

1. And when they are chosen who are set apart to receive baptism let their life be examined, whether they lived piously while catechumens, whether they 'honoured the widows', whether they visited the sick, whether they have fulfilled every good work.

2. If those who bring them bear witness to them that they have done thus, then let them hear the gospel . . .

7. Those who are to receive baptism shall fast on the Preparation [Friday] and on the Sabbath [Saturday]. And on the Sabbath the bishop shall assemble those who are to be baptized in one place, and shall bid them all to pray and bow the knee.

8. And laying his hand on them he shall exorcise every evil spirit to flee away from them and never to return to them

henceforward. And when he has finished exorcising, let him breathe on their faces and seal their foreheads and ears and noses and then let him raise them up.

9. And they shall spend all the night in vigil, reading the scriptures to them and instructing them.

It will be noticed just how seriously the early Church took the biblical teaching concerning the power and influence of Satan in the world and upon people. He had to be exorcised in the name of Jesus.

Secondly, here are the instructions for the actual baptism. They include testing for genuine repentance and true faith.

1. And at the hour when the cock crows they shall first [of all] pray over the water.

2. When they come to the water, let the water be pure and flowing.

3. And they shall put off their clothes.

4. And they shall baptize the little children first. And if they can answer for themselves, let them answer. But if they cannot, let their parents answer or someone from their family.

5. And next they shall baptize the grown men; and last the women, who shall have loosed their hair and laid aside their gold ornaments. Let no one go down to the water having any alien object with them.

6. And at the time determined for baptizing, the bishop shall give thanks over the oil and put it into a vessel and it is called the Oil of Thanksgiving . . .

9. And when the presbyter takes hold of each one of those who are to be baptized, let him bid him renounce saying:

I renounce thee, Satan, and all thy service and all thy works.

10. And when he has said this let him anoint with the Oil of Exorcism, saying:

Let all evil spirits depart far from thee.

11. Then after these things let him give over to the presbyter who stands at the water. And let them stand in the water naked. And let a deacon likewise go down with him into the water.

12. And he goes down to the water, let him who baptizes lay hand on him saying thus:

Dost thou believe in God the Father Almighty?

13. And he who is being baptized shall say:
I believe.

14. Let him forthwith baptize him once, having his hand laid upon his head.

15. And after [this] let him say:
Dost thou believe in Christ Jesus, the Son of God
Who was born of Holy Spirit and the Virgin Mary,
Who was crucified in the days of Pontius Pilate,
And died,
And rose the third day living from the dead
And ascended into the heavens,
And sat down at the right hand of the Father,
And will come to judge the living and the dead?

16. And when he says: *I believe*, let him baptize him the second time.

17. And again let him say:
Dost thou believe in the Holy Spirit in the Holy Church, And the resurrection of the flesh?

18. And he who is being baptized shall say: *I believe*. And so let him baptize him the third time.

19. And afterwards when he comes up he shall be anointed with the Oil of Thanksgiving saying:
I anoint thee with holy oil in the Name of Jesus Christ.

20. And so each one drying himself they shall now put on their clothes, and after this let them be together in the assembly.

Finally, there is the laying on of hands and anointing with oil symbolising the descent and infilling of the Spirit.

1. And the bishop shall lay his hand upon them invoking and saying:
O Lord God, who didst count these worthy of deserving the forgiveness of sins by the laver of regeneration, make them worthy to be filled with thy Holy Spirit and send upon them thy grace, that they may serve thee according to thy will; to thee is the glory, to the Father and to the Son with the Holy Ghost in the holy Church, both now and ever and world without end. Amen.

2. After this pouring the consecrated oil and laying his hand on his head, he shall say:
I anoint thee with holy oil in God the Father Almighty and Christ Jesus and the Holy Ghost.

3. And sealing him on the forehead, he shall give him the kiss of peace and say:

The Lord be with you.

And he who has been sealed shall say:

And with thy spirit.

4. And so shall he do to each one severally.

5. Thenceforward they shall pray together with all the people. But they shall not previously pray with the faithful before they have undergone these things.

6. And after the prayers, let them give the kiss of peace.

Then followed the Eucharist and first partaking of Holy Communion. (The translation is taken from the edition published by Gregory Dix, *The Apostolic Tradition*, ed. G. Dix, 1937.)

Since the work of God in regenerating the soul is secret and invisible, it is impossible to claim that in each and every case God's grace filled the heart at the same time as the baptism in water and anointing with oil occurred. What is clear is that baptism was such a tremendous experience that it was not easily forgotten – and so highly was it thought of that not a few theologians in the early Church had great difficulty in thinking how there could be further forgiveness of sins on earth after the 'washing' and 'purification' of baptism.

Comments

According to modern, popular evangelical teaching and understanding, many (perhaps all) who were sponsored to enter the catechumenate in the early centuries were actually 'converted'. That is, they had made a decision to follow Jesus Christ, or, at least, to make the most serious and solemn enquiries concerning him and his way.

Yet, as we have seen, the leadership of the Church in the early centuries did not see it this way. It looked for evidence of genuine repentance and faith over a period of time: it sought to develop and nurture the interest and commitment of the catechumens before bringing their turning to God through Christ to a climax in the administration of the Lord's sacrament of holy baptism. When we recall the interpretation of the parable of the sower provided by Jesus (Mark 4:10ff.), we can appreciate the need for care. Not all who receive the Gospel continue to live by it as disciples of Jesus – they are like the seed falling on the hard path, in rocky places and among thorns. Further, the need for care was intensified by the real belief in the power of Satan over people. In the catechumenate the hold of Satan over disciples had to be broken through exorcism in the name of Jesus.

So the idea of conversion as being a turning around to walk with Christ to God and having its fulfilment and climax in baptism makes good sense. So much so, that at the reforming Council of the RC Church (Vatican II) the assembled bishops made the decision to revive the catechumenate for all who wished to enter the Church as adult believers. Here is an extract from the *Decree on the Church's Missionary Activity* (1965). It repays careful reading.

> Those who have received from God the gift of faith in Christ, through the Church, should be admitted with liturgical rites to the catechumenate which is not a mere exposition of dogmatic truths and norms of morality, but a period of formation in the whole Christian life, an apprenticeship of sufficient duration, during which the disciples will be joined to Christ their teacher. The catechumens should be properly initiated into the mystery of salvation and the practice of the evangelical virtues, and they should be introduced into the life of faith, liturgy and charity of the People of God by successive sacred rites.
>
> Then, having been delivered from the powers of darkness through the sacraments of Christian initiation (cf. Col. 1:13), and having died, been buried, and risen with Christ (cf. Rom. 6:4–11; Col. 2:12–13; 1 Pet. 3:21–22; Mk. 16:16), they receive the Spirit of adoption of children (cf. 1 Th. 3:5–7; Acts 8:14–17)

and celebrate with the whole people of God the memorial of the Lord's death and resurrection.

It is desirable that the liturgy of Lent and Paschal time should be restored in such a way that it will serve to prepare the hearts of the catechumens for the celebration of the Paschal Mystery, at whose solemn ceremonies they are reborn to Christ in baptism.

This Christian initiation, which takes place during the catechumenate, should not be left entirely to the priests and catechists, but should be the concern of the whole Christian community, especially of the sponsors, so that from the beginning the catechumens will feel that they belong to the people of God. Since the life of the Church is apostolic, the catechumens must learn to cooperate actively in the building up of the Church and in its work of evangelization, both by the example of their lives and the profession of their faith (*Vatican Council II*, ed. Austin Flannery O.P., p. 828).

In the context of the rediscovery of the Bible by Catholics, this revival of the catechumenate is proving of great evangelistic benefit both in the developed and developing countries.

Not only Roman Catholics but Lutherans and Anglicans are also making moves to revive the adult catechumenate. Often this is happening because, having first revived the special services of Easter Eve and Easter Day, parishes are recognising that Lent is an excellent time both to prepare candidates for baptism and, for those baptised as infants, to renew their baptismal vows.

Personally I believe that the revival of the catechumenate is an excellent move. Where it is well managed with good discipline and sound teaching, it will be a great boon. My only fear is that it will become a playground for those who love ceremonial and liturgy more than they love evangelism and teaching. It is no good reviving ancient liturgies, rites, ceremonies and customs unless with them comes the commitment and power that accompanied them when they were first created.

6

THE PROTESTANT MODEL

As used in the popular press today the word 'Protestant' has a negative image. It points to a hard-line right-wing opponent of Roman Catholicism and reasonable religion. Such a meaning is much in contrast to its original meaning as used in the sixteenth century. From 1529 at the Second Diet of Spires in Germany, it referred to those who made this declaration: 'We are determined by God's grace and aid to abide by God's Word alone, the Holy Gospel contained in the biblical books of the Old and New Testaments. This Word alone should be preached, and nothing contrary to it. It is the only Truth. It is the sure rule of all Christian doctrine and conduct. It can never fail or deceive us.' Thus it is not a protest *against* but rather a protest *for*: it is a declaration of faithfulness to the Gospel of our Lord Jesus Christ and devotion to his person. Thus the word is used in this chapter in its original meaning of 'one who protests for the Gospel'.

In the early sixteenth century, there was a tremendous shake-up of the Christian Church in Western Europe. The one medieval Catholic Church, under the ultimate authority of the Pope in Rome, found itself losing the allegiance of national and provincial churches. These claimed to be undergoing a reformation and renewal according to the Gospel and Word of God: they became Protestant

Churches. This movement for change was led by such men as Martin Luther, John Calvin and Thomas Cranmer, to name three of the best known of a large group of reformers.

We turn our attention in this chapter to the teaching of Luther, Calvin and Cranmer, which despite differences in emphasis, belongs to the same general framework. In the medieval Church the word *conversion* (Latin, *conversio*), had been used to describe the act of taking up the celibate life to become a monk or nun. As we shall see, the Protestant Reformers used the word to describe the internal action of God upon and in the soul of man, leading to a life of dedication to Jesus Christ. Their teaching on conversion applied to all people (not merely a select few) and was worked out in the context of the practice of universal infant baptism.

The Reformers did not hesitate in their continuation of the practice of baptising babies because they believed that they were doing the equivalent in the new covenant of what the Jews did in the old covenant in the practice of circumcising infant boys. Instead of the original apostolic practice of baptism following repentance and faith, they sought to interpret the Gospel within a structure which began with the act of baptism. They taught baptism followed by or growing into repentance and faith. Conversion could occur in childhood or adulthood.

Martin Luther (1483–1546)

Martin Luther was baptised as a baby and later entered a monastery before becoming a teacher of theology in the new University of Wittenburg, Germany. He took the calling to be a Christian and a monk most seriously and, in doing so, found the teaching he received from within the Church unsatisfactory with respect to his own personal search for salvation from God. Not that he did not try to fulfil all the religious duties imposed upon and recommended to him! He was over-diligent! Through them, however, he could find no peace in his heart and no sense of being forgiven by God and delivered from fear of divine wrath. Deliverance came to him as he paid more and more attention to the New Testament and especially to the teaching of the apostle Paul in Romans and Galatians.

Here is how he described his attainment of an assurance of salvation and of being in a right relationship with God-in-Christ. In the preface to the complete edition of his Latin writings published in 1545 he looked back to his experience over twenty-five years earlier:

> I greatly longed to understand Paul's Epistle to the Romans and nothing stood in the way but one expression, 'the justice of God,' because I took it to mean that justice whereby God is just and deals justly in punishing the unjust. My situation was that, although an impeccable monk, I stood before God as a sinner troubled in conscience, and I had no confidence that my merit would assuage him. Therefore I did not love a just and angry God, but rather hated and murmured against him. Yet I clung to the dear Paul and had a great yearning to know what he meant.
>
> Night and day I pondered until I saw the connection between the justice of God and the statement that 'the just shall live by his faith.' Then I grasped that the justice of God is that righteousness by which through grace and sheer mercy God justifies us through faith. Thereupon I felt myself to be reborn and to have gone through open doors into paradise. The whole of Scripture took on a new meaning, and whereas before the justice of God had filled me with hate, now it became to me inexpressibly sweet in great love. This passage of Paul became to me a gate to heaven.

True to this powerful experience of the God of all grace, Luther passionately taught for the rest of his life the need to believe the Gospel and be placed in a right relationship with God (justification by faith). He believed that where the

Gospel was clearly proclaimed people would come to genuine faith more quickly and with less difficulty than had been his own way to peace with God.

Luther had a very high view of baptism as a sacrament instituted by Christ and he had no hesitation in seeing the baptism of infants as wholly in accord with the mind of Christ. He makes this clear in his *The Large Catechism* (1529), which contains a lengthy exposition of baptism. 'To be baptised in God's name is to be baptised not by men but by God himself. Although it is performed by men's hands, it is nevertheless truly God's own act.' God's faithful and true Word is joined to the water so that he who believes and is baptised receives most surely God's salvation, including the gift of the indwelling Spirit.

Luther held that baptism, once administered, was valid for all time and thus whenever faith arose in the heart then the efficacy of baptism came into effect. He believed that some infants were able, in a mysterious but real way, to trust in Christ at their baptism and receive there and then the gift of the indwelling Spirit and be placed in a right relationship with God. He also held that some infants only believed vicariously through their sponsors (godparents) and exercised true personal faith later in life. Luther was not, it seems, too bothered at what precise moment a baptised child began to trust in God as the God of all grace; what interested him more was living a life in the strength and meaning of holy baptism. This is how he expressed it in *The Large Catechism*:

> We must know what Baptism signifies and why God ordained just this sign and external observance for the sacrament by which we are first received into the Christian Church. This act or observance consists in being dipped into the water, which covers us completely, and being drawn out again. These two parts, being dipped under the water and emerging from it, indicate the power and effect of Baptism, which is simply the slaying of the old Adam and the resurrection of the new man,

both of which actions must continue in us our whole life long. Thus a Christian life is nothing else than a daily Baptism, once begun and ever continued. For we must keep at it incessantly, always purging out whatever pertains to the old Adam, so that whatever belongs to the new man may come forth. What is the old man? He is what is born in us from Adam, irascible, spiteful, envious, unchaste, greedy, lazy, proud, yes and unbelieving: he is beset with all vices and by nature has nothing good in him. Now, when we enter Christ's kingdom, this corruption must daily decrease so that the longer we live the more gentle, patient, and meek we become, and the more free from greed, hatred, envy and pride.

Therefore each day the Christian, in the strength of the Holy Spirit, is to believe afresh the promises of the Gospel and follow Christ and, at the same time, he is to set aside and reject what he knows, through the Law and by the Gospel to be unacceptable and unpleasing to God. Thus, while the internal renewal by God's action and presence occurs in relation to water baptism, the living daily in the knowledge that 'I have been baptised' is the secret of true Christian faith, hope and love.

The *internal* action of God in the soul, affecting heart, mind and will, was called conversion by Luther. Conversion meant the inner illumination of the mind, the bending of the will towards God and the infusion of the love of God in the heart. This is clear in certain theological debates within the German Evangelical (Lutheran) Church both during and after Luther's lifetime. One debate was concerning how, if at all, a sinner co-operates with God in this *conversion*. Now Luther and every Lutheran held that a believer co-operates with God in the sense that he makes use of God's help in his daily attempt to live as a baptised Christian. But is there co-operation in the initial act of internal conversion/renewal/regeneration which normally takes place in relation to holy baptism? To this Luther and orthodox Lutherans gave a clearly negative answer. Perhaps in no Lutheran document is this 'No' made clearer than in the *Formula of Concord* (1577). Here are two brief extracts:

> Just as little as a person who is physically dead can by his own powers prepare or accommodate himself to regain temporal life, so little can a man who is spiritually dead, in sin, prepare or address himself by his own power to obtain spiritual and heavenly righteousness and life, unless the Son of God has liberated him from the death of sin and made him alive.

> In his own conversion or regeneration he can as little begin, effect, or co-operate in anything as a stone, a block, or a lump of clay could. Although he can direct the members of his body, can hear the Gospel and meditate on it to a certain degree, and can even talk about it . . . yet he considers it folly and cannot believe it.

Therefore there is no co-operation with God in conversion/ regeneration/inner renewal. It is a divine work and a divine work only. However,

> after God, through the Holy Spirit in Baptism, has kindled and wrought a beginning of true knowledge of God and faith, we ought to petition him incessantly that by the same Spirit and grace, through daily exercise in reading his Word and putting it into practice, he would preserve faith and his heavenly gifts in us and strengthen us daily until our end.

Lutherans were well aware that not all the baptised lived as the baptised ought to live. 'If those who have been baptised act contrary to their conscience and permit sin to rule in themselves and thus grieve the Holy Spirit within them and lose him, they dare not be baptised again, though they must certainly be converted again.' In other words the Holy Spirit must return to a baptised person for that person to be turned towards God in true conversion. For

> in true conversion there must be a change, there must be new activities and emotions in the intellect, will and heart, so that the heart learns to know sin, to fear the wrath of God, to turn from

sin, to understand and accept the promise of grace in Christ, to have good spiritual thoughts, Christian intentions, and diligence, and to fight against the flesh, etc. For if none of these things takes place, there is no true conversion.

Thus the Lutheran scheme is baptism (including internal conversion) leading to a life of repentance and faith, which may be interrupted by backsliding thus requiring conversion again. The quality of Christian living is, of course, not only related to the divine initiative and human response but also to the quality of the teaching and church life into which the child is baptised. True penitence and living faith are more likely to be the fruit of baptism in a church where the Gospel is faithfully preached than one where it is dimly or half-heartedly proclaimed. So the authentic Lutheran emphasis is on the preaching of the Gospel and the response of faith, leading to a Christian life which is an outworking of the grace and meaning of holy baptism.

Luther, himself, never produced a service of confirmation to complement his revised service of baptism (1526). He believed that young people should be well instructed in the faith (hence his *Small* and *Large Catechisms*) and then examined by their pastor before being admitted to Holy Communion. After his death, however, the rite of confirmation was introduced within the Lutheran churches primarily for young people. It came at the end of a period of preparation and was seen as a formal way of personally confessing that faith, originally confessed for them by their godparents in infant baptism.

John Calvin (1509–64)

Calvin was a Frenchman who revealed little of his inner life and who would have preferred the life of a scholarly recluse to that of a public pastor, preacher and reformer. In a rare glimpse into his own spiritual pilgrimage, he wrote this in his preface to the *Commentary on the Psalms* (1557):

> My father intended me as a young boy for theology. But when he saw that the science of law made those who cultivate it wealthy, he was led to change his mind by the hope of material gain for me. So it happened that I was called back from the study of philosophy to learn law. I followed my father's wish and attempted to do faithful work in this field; but God, by the secret leading of his providence, turned my course another way.
>
> First, when I was too firmly addicted to the papal superstitions to be drawn easily out of such a deep mire, by a sudden conversion God brought my mind (already more rigid than suited my age) to submission to him. I was so inspired by a taste of true religion and I burned with such a desire to carry my study further, that although I did not drop other subjects, I had no zeal for them. In less than a year, all who were looking for a purer doctrine began to come to learn from me, although I was a novice and a beginner.

Here Calvin tells how as a young man, a devout Roman Catholic, he experienced an inner change which brought an illumination of mind and a thirst for more knowledge of God and experience of his grace. Conversion, here as elsewhere in Calvin's writings, is the work of God in bringing new life to the soul and beginning the task of renewing the image of God there.

Like Luther, Calvin had been baptised as an infant, but what he judged to be his authentic Christian experience only began when he was a student. However, Calvin (like Luther) did not make his own experience to be that which others ought to follow. His whole thinking about turning to God-in-Christ began from his insights into the doctrine of election in Christ unto salvation. His teaching is clearly presented in his *Institutes*. Thus, while all were to be baptised as infants the divine work of regeneration/conversion/renewal of the divine image would only begin and continue in the elect (whose identity God alone knew). Pastorally

Calvin treated all as potentially the elect of God and so in baptismal preparation and services of baptism, as well as in preaching and counselling, he urged people to repent of their sins and to believe in and follow Christ.

While Luther and Lutherans gave the impression that divine regeneration was likely to occur at baptism, Calvin and the Calvinists were less certain of the new birth/internal conversion occurring at infant baptism, even where the sponsors and parents were wholehearted believers. In Article 20 of the *Consensus Tigurinus* (the Zurich Agreement) written by Calvin before 1551, we read the following:

> The benefit which we receive from the sacraments should by no means be restricted to the time in which they are administered to us; just as if the visible sign, when brought forward into view, did at the same moment bring God's grace with itself. For those who are baptised in early infancy, God regenerates in boyhood, in budding youth and sometimes even in old age. So the benefit of baptism lies open to the whole course of life; for the promise that it contains is perpetually valid.

Calvin did not envisage that anyone truly regenerated/ converted by God would ever need to be reconverted and re-renewed. Certainly he took the possibility of backsliding into account; but for him inner conversion was God's work in the elect, and in the elect only, and thus once regenerate, always regenerate. As a result of this internal, secret work of the Spirit, the individual is united to Christ in faith and love and desires to know God and to do his will. Thus inner conversion leads to a practical turning to God, in a life of repentance, faith, hope and love.

Calvin held that in the context of the worship and preaching of the Church the elect were united by the Holy Spirit to the exalted Lord Jesus Christ and as a result of that spiritual/heavenly union faith arose in their hearts and they looked to Christ for salvation, while, at the same time, the work of inner renewal of the soul (mind, heart and will) began. Conversion was the word Calvin used particularly of the bending or directing of the human will to will what God desires and commends.

Though Calvin believed in instantaneous spiritual union with Christ, leading to the impartation of divine life into the soul, he did not teach that the result of this internal, spiritual and non-experiential activity would be known and felt at once. The turning to God, initiated by the secret work of the Holy Spirit, could occur slowly or quickly and at any age from childhood to old age. What was important for him was living the Christian life as a result of inner renewal and conversion; this is the life of repentance, the life of mortifying sin and living in Christ unto God, and the life of imitating Christ in the strength of the Spirit. This life is the life of faith, looking unto Christ and trusting in the promises of God concerning Christ and salvation.

This teaching of Calvin is faithfully reproduced – howbeit in a controversial situation – by the Reformed or Calvinist divines who met at the Synod of Dort in 1618. They had the following to say about conversion or regeneration as the work of God within the elect, in Chapter 3 of their Statement:

ARTICLE 11

How God Brings About Conversion

When God, moreover, carries out His good pleasure in the elect, or works in them true conversion, He not only sees to it that the gospel is outwardly preached to them, powerfully enlightening their minds by the Holy Spirit so that they may rightly understand and discern the things of the Spirit of God, but by the effectual working of that same regenerating Spirit He also penetrates into the innermost recesses of man, opens the closed and softens the hard heart, circumcises that which was uncircumcised, and pours new qualities into the will. He makes the will which was dead alive, which was bad good, which was unwilling willing, which was stubborn obedient, and moves and strengthens it so that, like a good tree, it may be able to produce the fruits of good works.

ARTICLE 12

The Supernatural Character of Regeneration

And this is that regeneration, that new creation, that resurrection from the dead, that making alive, so highly spoken of in the Scriptures, which God works in us without our help. But this regeneration is by no means brought about only by outward teaching or preaching, by moral persuasion, or by such a method of working that after God has done His work, it remains in the power of man to be regenerated or not regenerated, converted or not converted. It is, however, clearly a supernatural, most powerful and at the same time most delightful, marvelous, secret, and inexpressible work which, according to the Scriptures inspired by the Author of regeneration, is not inferior in power to creation or the resurrection of the dead. Hence all those in whose hearts God works in this amazing way are certainly, unfailingly, and effectually regenerated and do actually believe. Therefore the will so renewed is not only acted upon and moved by God but, acted upon by God, the will itself also acts. Hence also man himself, through the grace he has received, is rightly said to believe and repent.

In this important and influential Statement we encounter the clear doctrine that only those who are the elect of God will actually be inwardly (as well as outwardly) called by God and thus truly converted and actually genuinely repent and believe. Since would-be communicants were examined by the pastor before admission to Holy Communion, only the converted were expected to participate fully in the life of the Church.

Thomas Cranmer (1489–1556)

Thomas Cranmer, who became Archbishop of Canterbury, is less well known than either Martin Luther or John

Calvin. No school of theology and no denomination is named after him, but his role as the major architect of the reformed liturgy of the Church of England and of its confession of faith (the Thirty-Nine Articles) does bear comparison with the work of either Luther or Calvin, especially when it is borne in mind that the Anglican Communion of Churches, like Lutheranism and Presbyterianism (Calvinism), is a universal denomination.

If Cranmer had a crisis experience in terms of his growth into the full freedom of being justified by faith, we do not know of it. What we do know is that in the 1520s, while at Cambridge University as a Fellow of Jesus College, he made a serious study of the New Testament and carefully examined the new 'Lutheran' doctrines that were beginning to be known in England. He came to reject the traditional, medieval doctrine that justification is a process of being made just/righteous in favour of the teaching of Luther that justification is an act of God pardoning and accepting the believing sinner. This principle of justification by faith is to be found within all the major texts, liturgical and doctrinal, that he produced for the reformed catholicity which the Church of England sought to embody when he was the archbishop. Cranmer was the one primarily responsible for the Book of Common Prayer (1549; revised 1552), containing all the services of the Church, together with a catechism; and for the Articles of Religion (1553); as well as a book of sermons to be read in parish churches known as the *First Book of Homilies* (1547).

Before looking at the concept of conversion in the Formularies of the Church of England, it will perhaps be useful to note the use of the noun, 'conversion', and the verb 'to convert'. In the Book of Common Prayer of 1552 we find that the noun is used to describe one of the 'holy' days, 'The Conversion of St Paul'. In the collect for this day we find the petition to God: 'Grant, we beseech thee, that we, having his wonderful conversion in remembrance, may shew forth our thankfulness unto thee for the same, by following the holy doctrine which he taught . . .' Further, the verb appears in the third collect for Good Friday. 'O merciful God, who hast made all men, and hatest nothing that thou hast made, nor wouldest the death of a sinner, but rather that he should be converted and live; have mercy upon all Jews, Turks, Infidels, and Heretics, and take from them all ignorance, hardness of heart, and contempt of thy Word . . .' In both these cases, which are the only examples, the intention is probably that God is the agent of conversion. There was a minor revision of this Prayer Book in 1661/2, leading to what has become the definitive edition of 1662. In the new preface of this edition we find that an explanation is offered for the additional service entitled, 'The ministration of Baptism to such as are of riper years and able to answer for themselves'. In this explanation the verb 'to convert' is used. This rite will not only be useful for those who, because of the spread of Anabaptist views, have not been baptised as infants, but also for 'the baptising of natives in our plantations, and others converted to the faith'.

Apart from these three examples, the only other place where the noun or verb occurs in the official Church of England Formularies is in the Homily of Repentance, found in the *Second Book of Homilies* (1563). Here Christ is presented as the only one 'by whom we may be able to convert' to God; repentance is described as 'the conversion or turning again of the whole man unto God' and also as 'a full conversion to God in a new life, to glorify his name'. Bishop John Jewel was responsible for the editing of this *Second Book*, just as Cranmer had been responsible for the *First Book*. In this Homily of Repentance conversion is used not in the passive but in the active sense of what sinners do in response to the Gospel and with the help of God. This active usage of 'convert' anticipates the later English Puritan use of conversion as the turning to God in repentance and faith. This Homily was, of course, addressed to people sitting in

parish churches who had been baptised as infants and it is a
serious call to all, whether committed or nominal believers,
to see repentance – a wholehearted turning to God and
forsaking of sin – as at the heart of the Christian life and
indissolubly linked to faith.

But to return now to Cranmer and the services for which
he was responsible. The structure he created in which he
believed that God's converting the sinner and the sinner's
converting to God could take place was quite simple. It was
infant baptism, supported and followed by Christian nurture, leading to confirmation, where a public confession of
faith and commitment to Christ was made. Then as young
people (teenagers) those confirmed were to hear the Word
of God preached and to receive the sacrament of the Lord's
Supper. This structure allowed for God's act of regene-
ration/conversion to occur with or after baptism, and the
human response to be gradual or sudden. Thus Cranmer
committed the Church of England to a Catholic doctrine of
baptism and a Protestant doctrine of justification by faith.

After the baptism of the infant the minister was required
to offer this prayer of thanksgiving to God:

> We yield thee hearty thanks, most merciful Father, that it hath
> pleased thee to regenerate *this Infant* with thy holy Spirit, to
> receive *him* for thine own *Child* by adoption, and to incorporate
> *him* into thy holy Church. And humbly we beseech thee to
> grant, that *he*, being dead unto sin, and living unto righteous-
> ness, and being buried with Christ in his death, may crucify the
> old man, and utterly abolish the whole body of sin; and that,
> as *he is* made *partaker* of the death of thy Son, *he* may also be
> *partaker* of his resurrection . . .

Having completed the prayer, the minister then gave this
exhortation to the godparents:

> Forasmuch as *this Child hath* promised by you *his* sureties to
> renounce the devil and all his works, to believe in God, and to
> serve him; ye must remember, that it is your parts and duties to

see that *this Infant* be taught, so soon as *he* shall be able to learn, what a solemn vow, promise, and profession, *he hath* here made by you. And that *he* may know these things the better, ye shall call upon *him* to hear Sermons; and chiefly ye shall provide, that *he* may learn the Creed, the Lord's Prayer, and the Ten Commandments, in the vulgar tongue, and all other things which a Christian ought to know and believe to his soul's health; and that *this Child* may be virtuously brought up to lead a godly and a christian life; remembering always, that Baptism doth represent unto us our profession; which is, to follow the example of our Saviour Christ, and to be made like unto him; that, as he died, and rose again for us, so should we, who are baptized, die from sin, and rise again unto righteousness; continually mortifying all our evil and corrupt affections, and daily proceeding in all virtue and godliness of living.

When we move on to the Order of Confirmation we find that it has two parts: the first is a personal confession of faith by the one to be confirmed and the second is the act of confirmation performed by the bishop. Thus confirmation was administered only to those who were old enough to be able to understand the basic teaching of the Apostles' Creed and to dedicate themselves to God. The actual confirming by the bishop consisted of two prayers, the second one said by him as he laid his hands upon the head of the candidate.

The first prayer recalls the infant baptism and prays that the candidates may be strengthened by the Holy Spirit:

Almighty and everliving God, who hast vouchsafed to regenerate these thy servants by Water and the holy Ghost, and hast given unto them forgiveness of all their sins; Strengthen them, we beseech thee, O Lord, with the Holy Ghost the Comforter, and daily increase in them thy manifold gifts of grace; the spirit of wisdom and understanding; the spirit of counsel and ghostly strength; the spirit of knowledge and true godliness; and fill them, O Lord, with the spirit of thy holy fear, now and for ever. *Amen.*

The second prayer, offered while the candidate kneels in front of the bishop, is the climax not only of the Order of Confirmation but also of the earlier rite of infant baptism.

Defend, O Lord, this thy Child [or *this thy Servant*] with thy
heavenly grace, that *he* may continue thine for ever; and daily
increase in thy holy Spirit more and more, until *he* come unto
thy everlasting kingdom. *Amen.*

According to Cranmer's desire and structure, each confirmed young person should be a converted person, a true
believer in the Lord Jesus.

Comments

Over the centuries thousands of people have come to full
commitment to Jesus Christ through the experience of
preparation for confirmation (or full church membership).
Not all perhaps realised at the time that this was the case,
but, looking back, they saw that there was a genuine change
in their attitude and direction of life from that period. What
their sponsors had promised on their behalf in infant baptism, they were now readily and gladly seeking to put into
practice in daily life. Whether or not they used the word
conversion (let us remember that choice of words depends
upon the type of language used in the church fellowship to
which one belongs), they were now converted. We need not
speculate as to the precise time of their internal conversion
(regeneration, inner renewal by the Spirit), but we can
accept that the gift of the Spirit is related to baptism and that
the two events need not occur simultaneously. In fact no
one can definitely state when he or she was internally born
again by the Spirit, because this internal divine action is
secret and invisible. All that a person can testify to is his/her
change of life in obedience to Jesus Christ.

We may now ask, 'Does this Protestant model provide
for the apostolic strands or elements of genuine conversion?' Certainly Luther, Calvin and Cranmer would reply
in the affirmative. Further they would say that a sense of

conviction of sin, repentance, faith in Jesus, baptism and church membership, need not occur in any particular order. Where infants are concerned they are baptised into Christ before they can possibly be aware of sin, repent and actively trust in Jesus as Saviour and Lord. As we have seen, when a person is brought to confirmation he or she ought at this stage to be truly converted. If they are not then the Church has failed in its work of nurture and teaching.

One final comment. There is a tendency today to claim that 'Christian initiation is completed in baptism'. So in some Anglican parishes, for example, small children are given Holy Communion for they are seen as members of Christ and of his Church. It is possible, of course, that by the grace of God, such children will be converted – perhaps in a gradual way over the years of infancy and youth. On the other hand, the great value of confirmation from the human standpoint is that it provides not only for a period of intense instruction and examination but also for a public confession of faith. Psychologically the latter is very important for those who are baptised as infants.

7

THE PURITAN MODEL

As the name suggests, a Puritan was a person who wanted to purify the English Church of what he believed to be the remaining popish rites and ceremonies in order to fashion the national Church after the pattern provided in the sacred Scriptures. Further, he wanted to see each member sanctified so that the congregation in the parish was a company of visible saints, together with others desiring to be genuinely converted to God.

As a movement, Puritanism flourished in England from the end of the sixteenth through to the end of the seventeenth century (though from 1662 it was pushed outside the national Church to create Protestant Nonconformity); it also crossed the Atlantic into New England in America, where it was influential for at least a century.

Puritan theologians, parish ministers and parish lecturers (preachers who were not the legally instituted pastors), led by such men as William Perkins (1558–1602), William Ames (1576–1633), Robert Bolton (1572–1631), Thomas Hooker (1586–1647), John Preston (1587–1628) and Richard Sibbes (1577–1635), carefully set out and chartered the experience of conversion (meaning the total response of the repentant and believing sinner to the Gospel). No school of theology or movement for renewal/reformation has given so much attention to the workings of the Spirit in the soul and the human response to the call of God. In fact, the attempts to itemise the route from indifference to commitment, or from opposition to obedience, became too rigid. This meant that some genuine seekers had great worries because they could not fit their experience into the 'approved' scheme. The Puritan preachers and pastors not only preached concerning the way of conversion but they also visited their flocks and enquired into the state of their souls, acting as doctors of the soul. Like the Reformers, they administered infant baptism.

The word 'conversion' as generally used by Puritans, referred primarily to the active response of the soul to the Gospel. Certainly they held that this could only occur because of the passive experience of regeneration. However, unlike the first Protestant Reformers who tended to equate conversion with internal regeneration (in which the soul is passive) the Puritans saw conversion as the active response of the soul (in heart, mind and will) to the work of the Holy Spirit in and upon the soul in regeneration.

The general pattern

From a perusal of Puritan writings, autobiographical and sermonic, it is possible to see seven stages, or seven steps, overlapping but yet distinct, through which a person must normally pass in order to be sure that he has truly been converted. The period of time could be anything from a few weeks to a few years for the whole process to occur.

1. A person is indifferent, perhaps hostile, to the preaching of the Gospel and the idea of conversion. (This is a later evaluation: at the time the person probably saw himself as a decent person who feared God.)

2. This person begins to feel a sense of dissatisfaction with his religious state, and becomes aware of his failures to do what God commands. An internal struggle begins. The Law of God makes him aware of his sin and sinfulness.

3. Through the enlightenment of the Holy Spirit and the teaching of the Bible, he begins to gain spiritual understanding and to take seriously the duty of prayer, reading the Bible, attending worship and engaging in self-examination. Yet the Law of God still works upon his conscience.

4. His attitude, habits and actions are changed, but he is still experiencing an internal struggle and still at least half-believing that his own activity, good works and decency are acceptable to God. He may appear to others as converted, but he knows that he is not yet converted. He does not have the internal peace of knowing he is right with God and accepted by him.

5. Quite suddenly he has a deep, spiritual experience (which could take place anywhere at any time) in which he sees his sinfulness before God, his inability to save himself and the glorious provision of grace in Jesus Christ. He finds himself trusting in Christ and in Christ alone for salvation and peace and joy flooding his heart.

6. As a result of this crisis, he feels like a new person since the old struggle, insecurities and terrors (of the Law) have gone. He wants to praise God and serve him in his Church.

7. The life of sanctification, mortifying sin and living in the new life of the resurrected Christ, begins and thus a new struggle begins – that of a child of God resisting the devil and not giving in to the world, the flesh and the devil.

We may observe that internal regeneration or new birth (John 3:3) was held to occur during or near stage five.

It will be obvious that Puritan accounts of conversion cannot, by their very nature be short! A classic account is *Grace Abounding to the Chief of Sinners* (1666), John Bunyan's dramatic tale of his conversion and Christian experience.

Fascinating accounts are provided by Samuel Clarke in his *A General Martyrologie . . . whereunto are added the lives of sundry modern divines* (1651) and his *The Lives of Sundry Eminent Persons in the Later Age* (1683). Here, however, is the recorded experience of David Brainerd (1718–47) who was a pioneer missionary to the Red Indians and who had a 'Puritan conversion' right at the end of the American Puritan period. What follows is related to stages 4, 5 and 6 as given above; it is found in his *Diary*:

> I continued, as I remember, in this state of mind, from Friday morning till the Sabbath evening following, (July 12, 1739,) when I was walking again in the same solitary place, where I was brought to see myself lost and helpless, as before mentioned. Here, in a mournful melancholy state, I was attempting to pray; but found no heart to engage in that or any other duty; my former concern, exercise, and religious affections were now gone. I thought that the Spirit of God had *quite* left me; but still was not distressed; yet disconsolate, as if there was nothing in heaven or earth could make me happy. Having been thus endeavouring to pray – though, as I thought, very stupid and senseless – for near half an hour; then, as I was walking in a dark thick grove, *unspeakable glory* seemed to open to the view and apprehension of my soul. I do not mean any *external* brightness, for I saw no such thing; nor do I intend any imagination of a body of light, some where in the third heavens, or any thing of that nature; but it was a new inward apprehension or view that I had of *God*, such as I never had before, nor any thing which had the least resemblance of it. I stood still; wondered; and admired! I knew that I never had seen before any thing comparable to it for excellency and beauty; it was widely different from all the conceptions that ever I had of God, or things divine. I had no particular apprehension of any one person in the Trinity, either the Father, the Son, or the Holy Ghost; but it appeared to be *Divine glory*. My soul *rejoiced with joy unspeakable*, to see such a God, such a glorious divine Being; and I was inwardly pleased and satisfied, that he should be *God over all* for ever and ever. My soul was so captivated and delighted with the excellency, loveliness, greatness, and other perfections of God, that I was

even swallowed up in him; at least to that degree, that I had no thought (as I remember) at *first*, about my own salvation, and scarce reflected that there was such a creature as myself.

Thus God, I trust, brought me to a hearty disposition to *exalt him*, and set him on the throne, and principally and ultimately to aim at his honour and glory, as King of the universe. I continued in this state of inward joy, peace, and astonishment, till near dark, without any sensible abatement; and then began to think and examine what I had seen; and felt sweetly *composed* in my mind all the evening following. I felt myself in a new world, and every thing about me appeared with a different aspect from what it was wont to do. At this time, the *way of salvation* opened to me with such infinite wisdom, suitableness, and excellency, that I wondered I should ever think of any other way of salvation; was amazed that I had not dropped my own contrivances, and complied with this lovely, blessed, and excellent way before. If I could have been saved by my own duties, or any other way that I had formerly contrived, my whole soul would now have refused it. I wondered that all the world did not see and comply with this way of salvation, entirely by the *righteousness of Christ*.

The sweet relish of what I then felt, continued with me for several days, almost constantly, in a greater or less degree. – I could not but sweetly rejoice in God, lying down and rising up. The next Lord's day I felt something of the same kind, though not so powerful as before. But not long after I was again involved in *thick darkness*, and under great distress; yet not of the same kind with my distress under convictions. I was guilty, afraid, and ashamed to come before God; was exceedingly pressed with a sense of guilt: but it was not long before I felt, I trust, true repentance and joy in God. – About the latter end of August, I again fell under great darkness; it seemed as if the presence of God was *clean gone for ever*; though I was not so much distressed about my spiritual *state*, as I was at my being shut out from God's *presence*, as I then sensibly was. But it pleased the Lord to return graciously to me not long after.

It has been well said that David Brainerd was as a candle that burned brilliantly but briefly. He died before his thirtieth

birthday, but through his *Diary* he influenced thousands,
achieving more fame and spiritual influence in death than in
life.

We remarked above that not all those who believed that
they had experienced a genuine work of God in their souls
could trace their pilgrimage through every stage. For
example, Jonathan Edwards, the great New England
theologian, who so wanted to be converted to God in a full
and right way, wrote in his *Diary* when aged 19:

> The chief thing, that now makes me in any measure to question
> my good estate (before God), is my not having experienced
> conversion in those particular steps, wherein the people of New
> England, and anciently the Dissenters of Old England, used to
> experience it. Wherefore, now resolved, never to leave search-
> ing, till I have satisfyingly found out the very bottom and
> foundation, the real reason, why they used to be converted in
> those steps.

This quest for understanding concerning the way conversion to God occurs led him to write not a few books, of
which the most important was *A Treatise concerning Religious
Affections* (1746). What Edwards had not wholly experienced was what Puritans had called 'the work of humiliation', the deep conviction that he was wholly emptied of all
self and totally persuaded that he had no goodness of any
kind to offer to God. He had come straight from a sense of
need and of sin to an internal delight in God and his glory.
He described that delight in this way:

> The first instance, that I remember, of that sort of inward, sweet
> delight in God and divine things, that I have lived much in since,
> was on reading those words, 1 Tim. i. 17. *Now unto the King
> eternal, immortal, invisible, the only wise God, be honour and glory for ever
> and ever, Amen.* As I read the words, there came into my soul, and
> was as it were diffused through it, a sense of the glory of the
> Divine Being; a new sense, quite different from any thing I ever
> experienced before. Never any words of Scripture seemed to me

as these words did. I thought with myself, how excellent a Being that was, and how happy I should be, if I might enjoy that God, and be rapt up to him in heaven, and be as it were swallowed up in him for ever! I kept saying, and as it were singing, over these words of scripture to myself; and went to pray to God that I might enjoy him, and prayed in a manner quite different from what I used to do; with a new sort of affection. But it never came into my thought, that there was any thing spiritual, or of a saving nature in this.

From about that time, I began to have a new kind of apprehensions and ideas of Christ, and the work of redemption, and the glorious way of salvation by him. An inward, sweet sense of these things, at times, came into my heart; and my soul was led away in pleasant views and contemplations of them. And my mind was greatly engaged to spend my time in reading and meditating on Christ, on the beauty and excellency of his person, and the lovely way of salvation by free grace in him.

Such intellectual delight in God was a constant experience for Edwards throughout his life.

Richard Baxter

Baxter is one of the best-known and most widely read of English Puritan theologians of the seventeenth century. He was the minister of Kidderminster and his often reprinted *The Reformed Pastor* reveals his great care as a parish minister. Like Jonathan Edwards, Baxter also wanted to be able to record an experience of conversion which fitted into the established pattern. This did not happen and he recorded in his *Autobiography* how he had had doubts concerning his salvation, and that one of the chief causes of this was: 'Because I could not distinctly trace the workings of the Spirit upon my heart in that method which Mr Bolton, Mr Hooker, Mr Rogers and other divines prescribe . . .'

However, his own difficulties helped him the better to be a faithful pastor and preacher. He often taught his people the meaning of conversion and then gave them directions how to turn to God-in-Christ. His teaching is recorded in his *A Treatise of Conversion* (1657), *A Call to the Unconverted* (1657), *Now or Never* (1658) and *Directions and Persuasions to a sound Conversion* (1658). All these were written during his period at Kidderminster. We shall follow particularly the *Directions* in order to set out Baxter's teaching on conversion, addressed to ordinary churchgoers, baptised as infants.

He urged his parishioners to do the following (not all at the same time!).

1. Seek after a right understanding of the Gospel of God concerning Jesus Christ as well as why conversion is necessary. 'Ignorance is your disease,' he explained, 'and knowledge must be your cure.'

2. Carefully read the Bible every day, searching for understanding. 'Come to the Word in meekness and humility, with a teachable frame of spirit, a willingness to know the truth, a resolution to stand to it, and yield to what shall be revealed to you; beg of God to show you his will, to lead you into the truth, and you will find that he will be found of them that seek him.'

3. Seriously consider the great truths concerning God, Christ and yourself. 'Consideration opens the ear that was stopped, and the heart that was shut up; it sets the powers of the soul to work, and awakens it from the sleep of indifference and security.'

4. Ensure that God's work of humiliation within you is allowed to reach its conclusion. 'When your hearts begin to be afflicted for sin, go not among foolish and merry companions to drink or laugh it away; drive it not out of your minds, as unkindly, as if it came to do you hurt; but get alone, and consider of the matter, and on your knees in secret, beseech the Lord to follow it home, and break your hearts, and make you meet for his healing consolations; and

not to leave you in this red sea, but to bring you through and put the songs of praise into your mouths.'

5. Submit to Jesus Christ as Lord as he is offered to you in the Gospel. 'In this your Christianity consists, upon this your justification and salvation lie. This is the sum of your conversion, and the very heart of the new creature. The rest is all but the preparatives to this, or the fruit of it.'

6. Put to death your sinful nature and tear your heart away from affection for the world and its pleasures, for you cannot have God and mammon. 'Take yourselves as strangers here; and look on the world as a desolate wilderness, through which, in the communion of the militant saints, you may safely travel on to heaven; do not make it your home, nor take it for the smallest part of your felicity. To be sanctified without mortification is a palpable contradiction.'

7. Give yourself and all that you have to God. 'To be truly converted is to be called from things common and unclean, and separated to God; it is to be brought nigh to him, as the children of his household, that are themselves and all that they have, in his hands: it is to be taken off yourselves and your own, and to lose yourselves and all you have in God, by the most gainful loss.'

8. Be careful not to confuse a mere change in your opinions, outward profession and behaviour for true conversion. 'O what abundance of our poor neighbours would go to heaven, who are now on the way to hell, if an opinion that godliness is the wisest course, would serve the turn. If instead of conversion, God would take up with an opinion that they ought to turn; and if instead of a holy, heavenly life, God would accept of an opinion, that such are the happiest men that live such a life; and if instead of temperance, meekness, self-denial, and forgiving wrongs, God would accept of an opinion and confession that they should be temperate, meek and self-denying, and should forbear others and forgive them; then O what abundance would be saved, that are now in little hope of salvation.'

9. Fully acquaint yourself with the glory of the everlasting kingdom of heaven and make sure that you live in the light of your membership of that kingdom and your place in it. 'He that takes this world for his portion, and makes the felicity of it his end, is a carnal, worldly, unsanctified man, whatever good and godly actions may come in upon his mind. It is he, and only he, that is a sanctified believer, who looks on heaven as his only portion, and his sailing through the troublesome seas of this world, on purpose to come to that desired harbour; not loving those seas better than the land of rest, which he is sailing to; but patiently and painfully passing through them, because there is no other way to glory.'

10. Do not be satisfied that you are a true convert until God and his holy ways are your very love, desire and delight. 'Whom else can you love, if he [God] that is love itself seem not lovely to you? All loveliness is in him and from him, the creature hath none of it itself, nor for itself.'

11. To prevent the miscarriage of God's saving work within you, turn immediately to God in response to the Gospel. 'I beseech you, yea, as his messenger I charge you in his name, that you delay not an hour longer, but presently be resolved and make an unchangeable covenant with God; and as ever you would have favour in that day of your distress, delay not now to accept his favour, in the day of your visitation.'

12. Let your turning to God be without hesitation or reserve, well-grounded and of deliberate resolution. 'The resolution and vow of cleaving unto God in faith and holy obedience and of renouncing the flesh, the world and the devil; this is for all, and must be made and kept by all that will be saved.'

It would seem that Baxter did not expect people to seek to follow all of these directions at one and the same time. He well knew that to follow but three or four of them would be sufficient to ensure that a person was seriously seeking after God and wanting to experience his liberating and pardoning grace. Further, since the Puritans rejected the rite of confirmation, Baxter advocated that there be some opportunity for those who believed themselves to have been converted and who had satisfied their pastor of this fact, to make a public confession of faith and commitment before the whole congregation before entering into full church membership and partaking of the Lord's Supper.

Over in the free air of New England where Puritans were able to implement what they believed to be the right ordering of the Church of God, conversion (that is of those baptised as infants and already within the congregation but not the membership of the church) was made the door into receiving Holy Communion and full membership. This state of affairs helped, of course, to make people examine themselves and seek after the right experiences in order to ensure that they were truly converted and could persuade the pastor of this. Further, it led to the strange position of the infants born to the baptised who were not 'converted' members. There was much debate as to whether such children could be baptised – did they come within the promise of Acts 2:39 ('the promise is for you and your children . . .')?

Comments

The Puritan model of conversion was fully integrated into the life and witness of the local church. Its great strength was that it reflected the biblical concept that turning to God is the most important thing that can happen to a human being as he lives in God's world. It was closely related to a ministry of preaching, catechising in the home, family prayers and serious piety. However, in its more rigid form this model claimed too much in its delineation of the right (the only) process of conversion. It lacked flexibility in terms of its description of the way God chooses to bring a sinner to the life of holiness. It confused strands/elements with stages. In admitting this, we also have to recognise that those who were converted to God according to this model seem to have deeply and thoroughly converted, so that their lives were dominated by the passion to know, love and serve the Lord.

In the modern, Western world, where there is apparently little sense of sinning against God (because the sense of God as holy and as judge is very weak) there seem to be few people converted in a way that can be said to fit into the Puritan model. Especially missing from testimonies to conversion (even in 'Calvin' and 'Reformed' churches) is the deep and profound sense of being a sinner under the wrath of God and of feeling totally condemned by the holy Law of God. Perhaps this may be traced not only to the general ethos of our culture but also to the different styles and content of sermons today. This said – as I can sincerely testify – there is much to be gained by the study of Puritan literature on conversion and spirituality. I made great use of Richard Baxter's ideas in my *Longing for the Heavenly Realm* (Hodder, 1986), which shows that meditating upon Christ in glory is a spiritual duty and joy.

8

THE EVANGELISTIC MODEL

Mass evangelism in the modern era began when George Whitefield (1714–70) and John Wesley (1703–91) left the parish churches to preach to the crowds in churchyards, market-squares, grass fields and empty quarries. Then, in the early nineteenth century, through the example and teaching of Charles Finney (1792–1875), mass evangelism was given its distinctive form, the 'evangelistic model' of conversion was developed, and the Protestant and Puritan models of conversion laid aside. Most of us have encountered the evangelistic model by participating in or watching a Billy Graham evangelistic rally.

What the Puritans had expected would occur over a longish period – from weeks to months – Whitefield and Wesley came to believe could and did occur in minutes. These two English evangelists came to expect that not only instant regeneration/new birth but also instant conversion would occur if the Holy Spirit accompanied the preaching of the Gospel. Yet it took them some time to accept that the instantaneous conversion was as valid as that longer one, according to the Puritan or Protestant models (both of which taught instant yet invisible inner, spiritual regeneration).

Whitefield and the Wesleys

Obviously Whitefield reflected on this matter as this extract from one of his published sermons, 'The Conversion of Zacchaeus' (Luke 19:9–10), reveals. After having explained that apart from the call of Jesus (an 'external' call) Zacchaeus also experienced the call of/by the Spirit (an 'internal' call), and in response he had received Jesus and believed the Gospel, Whitefield made this observation about the time needed for conversion.

> It should seem that Zacchaeus was under soul distress but a little while . . . perhaps not so long as a quarter of an hour . . . for sometimes the Lord Jesus delights to deliver speedily. God is a sovereign agent, and works upon his children in their effectual calling, according to the counsel of his eternal will. It is with the spiritual, as the natural birth. All women have not like pangs: all Christians have not the like degree of conviction. But all agree in this, that all [converts] have Jesus Christ formed in their hearts: and those who have not so many trials at first may be visited with the great conflicts hereafter; though they never come into bondage again, after they have once received the spirit of adoption [Romans 8:14–15].

Here, of course, Whitefield is revising the Puritan model of conversion and saying that it is possible to have conflicts after rather than before genuine turning to God. And he suggested that Zacchaeus could have had such conflicts before he died.

For both Whitefield and Wesley, the embarking on evangelistic ministry which involved preaching to baptised (and often confirmed) people as if they were not already in some sense Christians meant also a rejection of the widely-held Anglican model of conversion through infant baptism and confirmation later in life. This rejection, often expressed more by default than by deliberate statement, led to much criticism from bishops and priests of the Church of England.

And it is easy to appreciate such criticism! It appeared that these itinerant evangelists put all their emphasis on the crisis experience of conversion followed by membership of religious societies (from which eventually grew the Methodist Church). Wesley, in particular, was a great organiser and he set up an elaborate system of fellowship groups for those who claimed to have been converted. However, had parish priests been more spiritually minded and diligent in duty, there would have been little need for all this.

From Charles Wesley, who was a great help to George Whitefield as he struggled to find true faith, came a tremendous volume of hymns which captured the theology and ethos of the evangelism and revival led by his brother, John, and Whitefield. Here is a hymn about conversion which illustrates its nature and the possibility that it may happen quickly.

Luke 14:16–24

1 Come, sinners, to the gospel feast,
   Let every soul be Jesu's guest;
   Ye need not one be left behind,
   For God hath bidden all mankind.

2 Sent by my Lord, on you I call,
   The invitation is to ALL:
   Come, all the world; come, sinner, thou!
   All things in Christ are ready now.

3 Come, all ye souls by sin opprest,
   Ye restless wanderers after rest,
   Ye poor, and maimed, and halt, and blind,
   In Christ a hearty welcome find.

4 Come, and partake the gospel feast;
   Be saved from sin; in Jesus rest;
   O taste the goodness of your God,
   And eat his flesh, and drink his blood!

5 Ye vagrant souls, on you I call;
   (O that my voice could reach you all!)
   Ye all may now be justified,
   Ye all may live, for Christ hath died.

6 My message as from God receive,
   Ye all may come to Christ, and live;
   O let his love your hearts constrain,
   Nor suffer him to die in vain!

7 His love is mighty to compel;
   His conquering love consent to feel,
   Yield to his love's resistless power,
   And fight against your God no more.

8 See him set forth before your eyes,
   That precious, bleeding sacrifice!
   His offered benefits embrace,
   And freely now be saved by grace.

9 This is the time; no more delay!
   This is the acceptable day,
   Come in, this moment, at his call,
   And live for him who died for all.

It is perhaps important to recognise that while Whitefield belonged to the Reformed/Calvinistic and the Wesleys to the Arminian/Laudian schools of theology, they did not differ as such on the doctrine of conversion. Their differences arose over the doctrines of predestination and entire sanctification.

One interesting fact about both the Wesleys and White-field is that their own, never-to-be-forgotten crisis experiences of gaining inward peace and joy and of beginning a harmonious and right relationship with God in commitment to Christ came at the end of a *long* period of dedicated, wholehearted searching. And though they were baptised and confirmed (even, in the case of the Wesleys, ordained) they did not see themselves as truly regenerated and converted persons until *after* these experiences.

Whitefield was the first to come to the great spiritual experience. As a member of Pembroke College, Oxford, he became a very serious-minded, religious young man, wholly involved in the so-called Oxford 'holy club', in which the Wesley brothers were prominent. As his hunger for right religion increased, so he found that despite all his efforts he could not find it. Reading the *Life of God in the Soul of Man* by Henry Scougal had a profound effect upon him.

God showed me that I must be born again, or be damned! I learned that a man may go to church, say his prayers, receive the sacrament, and yet not be a Christian. How did my heart rise and shudder, like a poor man that is afraid to look into his account-books, lest he should find himself a bankrupt.

'Shall I burn this book? Shall I throw it down? Or shall I search it?' I did search it; and, holding the book in my hand, thus addressed the God of heaven and earth: 'Lord, if I am not a Christian, or if I am not a real one, for Jesus Christ's sake, show me what Christianity is that I may not be damned at last!'

God soon showed me, for in reading a few lines further, that, 'true religion is a union of the soul with God, and Christ formed within us', a ray of Divine light was instantaneously darted in upon my soul, and from that moment, but not till then, did I know that I must become a new creature.

Thus began further intense searching, which involved physical illness and near exhaustion. Here is how Whitefield described the last part of this painful process in his *Journal*:

Soon after this, the holy season of Lent came on, which our friends kept very strictly, eating no flesh during the six weeks, except on Saturdays also, and ate nothing on the other days, except on Sunday, but sage-tea without sugar, and coarse bread. I constantly walked out in the cold mornings till part of one of my hands was quite black. This, with my continued abstinence, and inward conflicts, at length so emaciated my body, that, at Passion-week, finding I could scarce creep upstairs, I was obliged to inform my kind tutor of my condition, who immediately sent for a physician to me.

This caused no small triumph amongst the collegians, who began to cry out, 'What is his fasting come to now?' But I rejoiced in this reproach, knowing that, though I had been imprudent, and lost much of my flesh, yet, I had nevertheless increased in the Spirit.

This fit of sickness continued upon me for seven weeks, and a glorious visitation it was. The blessed Spirit was all this time purifying my soul. All my former gross and notorious, and even my heart sins also, were now set home upon me, of which I wrote down some remembrance immediately, and confessed them before God morning and evening. Though weak, I often spent two hours in my evening retirements, and prayed over my Greek Testament and Bishop Hall's most excellent *Contemplations*, every hour that my health would permit. About the end of the seven weeks, and after I had been groaning under an unspeakable pressure both of body and mind for about a twelve-month, God was pleased to set me free in the following manner. One day, perceiving an uncommon drought and a disagreeable clamminess in my mouth and using things to allay my thirst, but in vain, it was suggested to me, that when Jesus Christ cried out, 'I thirst,' His sufferings were near at an end. Upon which I cast myself down on the bed, crying out, 'I thirst! I thirst!' Soon after this, I found and felt in myself that I was delivered from the burden that had so heavily oppressed me. The spirit of mourning was taken from me, and I knew what it was truly to rejoice in God my Saviour; and, for some time, could not avoid singing psalms wherever I was; but my joy gradually became more settled, and, blessed be God, has abode and increased in my soul, saving a few casual intermissions, ever since.

Thus were the days of my mourning ended. After a long night of desertion and temptation, the Star, which I had seen at a distance before, began to appear again, and the Day Star arose in my heart. Now did the Spirit of God take possession of my soul, and, as I humbly hope, seal me unto the day of redemption.

Later, he would happily point out to friends the very place where, he believed, God gave him new birth into everlasting life.

John Wesley was baptised, confirmed and ordained and a foreign missionary before he found that peace of mind and joy of heart which ended his search for a right relationship with God and set him on the route to being an evangelist. It happened in a meeting of Moravians in the city of London, after Wesley had made their acquaintance on the ship that brought him back from America and his failed mission there. He had written in his *Journal*: 'I went to America to convert the Indians; but, oh, who shall convert me?' The answer was God working through the Moravians. Wesley has left a carefully prepared report of the day, May 24th, 1738, that God did this.

Early in the morning John opened his Greek New Testament where 2 Peter 1:4 seemed to stand out of the page: 'Whereby are given unto us exceeding great and precious promises . . .' (AV). A little later, before he left his room, the text ('You are not far from the kingdom of God') was impressed upon his heart. Later that day, he attended evensong at St Paul's Cathedral where the words of the anthem from Psalm 130:7 also deeply moved him: 'Let Israel hope in the Lord; for with the Lord there is mercy . . .' (AV). The climax came in the evening; he wrote in his *Journal*:

> In the evening I went very unwillingly to a society in Aldersgate Street, where one was reading Luther's preface to the *Epistle to the Romans*. About a quarter before nine, while he was describing the change which God works in the heart through faith in Christ, I felt my heart strangely warmed. I felt I did trust in Christ, Christ alone for salvation; and an assurance was given me that he had taken away *my* sins, even *mine*, and saved *me* from the law of sin and death.
>
> I began to pray with all my might for those who had in a more especial manner despitefully used me and persecuted me. I then testified openly to all there what I now first felt in my heart. But it was not long before the enemy suggested, 'This cannot be faith; for where is thy joy?' Then was I taught that peace and victory over sin are essential to faith in the Captain of our salvation; but that, as to the transports of joy that usually attend the beginning of it, especially in those who have mourned deeply, God sometimes giveth, sometimes withholdeth them.
>
> After my return home, I was much buffetted with temptations; but cried out, and they fled away. They returned again and again. I as often lifted up my eyes, and he 'sent me help from his holy place.' And herein I found the difference between this and my former state. I was striving, with all my might under the law, as well as under grace. But then I was sometimes, if not often, conquered; now, I was always conqueror.

The priest was now set to become the evangelist who would labour for nearly fifty years and travel around 250,000 miles, mostly on horseback.

Charles Wesley had had a similar experience a couple of days before, while lying in his bed with a sickness. John visited him late on the 24th, as Charles recorded: 'Towards ten my brother was brought in triumph by a troop of friends, and declared, "I believe!" We sang a hymn with great joy, and parted with prayer.' The hymn which

they sang had been written by Charles to celebrate his
own experience two days earlier and it was:

1 Where shall my wondering soul begin?
    How shall I all to heaven aspire?
A slave redeemed from death and sin,
    A brand plucked from eternal fire,
How shall I equal triumphs raise,
Or sing my great Deliverer's praise?

2 O how shall I the goodness tell,
    Father, which thou to me hast showed?
That I, a child of wrath and hell,
    I should be called a child of God,
Should know, should feel my sins forgiven,
Blest with this antepast of heaven!

3 And shall I slight my Father's love?
    Or basely fear his gifts to own?
Unmindful of his favours prove?
    Shall I, the hallowed cross to shun,
Refuse his righteousness to impart,
By hiding it within my heart?

4 No! though the ancient dragon rage,
    And call forth all his host to war,
Though earth's self-righteous sons engage,
    Them and their god alike I dare;
Jesus, the sinner's friend, proclaim;
Jesus, to sinners still the same.

5 Outcasts of men, to you I call,
    Harlots, and publicans, and thieves!
He spreads his arms to embrace you all;
    Sinners alone his grace receives;
No need of him the righteous have;
He came the lost to seek and save.

6 Come, O my guilty brethren, come,
  Groaning beneath your load of sin,
His bleeding heart shall make you room,
  His open side shall take you in;
He calls you now, invites you home;
Come, O my guilty brethren, come!

7 For you the purple current flowed
  In pardons from his wounded side,
Languished for you the eternal God,
  For you the Prince of glory died:
Believe, and all your sin's forgiven;
Only believe, and yours is heaven!

Already in this hymn the theme of evangelism is present and it is clear that for Whitefield and the Wesleys these crisis experiences of the grace of God in Jesus Christ served both to bring joy and peace to their hearts and a vision for evangelism to their minds.

Each of them later recorded various further powerful experiences of the presence of God and the outpouring of the Spirit. As soon as they began to preach, be it in cathedral, parish church, public place or churchyard, their preaching was effective and so blessed by God that people were deeply moved and began to profess deep and sincere conversion to God-in-Christ. They became the leaders of a revival movement in Britain and (especially in the case of Whitefield) important preachers in the revivals in the eastern part of America.

What was the basic content of their evangelistic message? It was (in summary):

God has provided salvation in and by Jesus Christ, who is the incarnate Son of God. He died in your place to bear the punishment due from God for your sins and he rose from the dead in order to gain for you a right relationship with God and eternal life with him. He is now enthroned at the right hand of the Father in heaven from where he rules his Church and pours out his Spirit upon his people. He also sends forth evangelists to preach the Gospel so that people may hear of what God commands them to do and to be. This Gospel is the good news that God has provided salvation from sin and eternal life. He calls upon people to repent of their sins, to forsake them and to believe on the Lord Jesus Christ for salvation. God offers to all who repent and believe the privilege of being made his children by adoption and also citizens of his heavenly kingdom.

This message was preached with great clarity and power and the hearers were urged, often dramatically so by White-field, who was a born actor, to act immediately in response to God's command and invitation. No long preparation was necessary! Here is a typical extract from Whitefield's *Journal*. The place is Philadelphia in America, the date is April 17th, 1740, and the preacher is still only 25 years of age.

I preached to upwards of ten thousand people, upon the woman who was cured of her bloody issue. Hundreds were graciously melted; and many, I hope, not only thronged around but also touched the Lord Jesus Christ by faith. About ten came to me after the sermon, under deep convictions, and told me the time when, and the manner how, the Lord Jesus made himself manifest to their souls. What gives me greater hope that this work is of God, is, because these convictions have remained on many since I was here last. Blessed be God, there is a most glorious work begun in this province. The Word of God everyday mightily prevails, and Satan loses ground. Lord Jesus, stretch out thy arm, and let not this work be stopped till we see that new Heaven and new Earth wherein dwelleth righteousness.

In America Whitefield left it to the local pastor(s) to care for the converts; but in Britain many were organised into fellowships (societies), first of all loosely connected with parish churches but later quite distinct (forming Method-ism). Only those with a genuine conversion experience to share were invited to join these societies.

So we see that the evangelical/evangelistic model of conversion that emerges in what are called the British Evangelical Revival and the Great Awakening in America, is that of a crisis experience, normally connected directly or indirectly with informed enthusiastic preaching. The event of conversion, which may be instant or extended, includes conviction for sin, repentance for sin and a turning to God so as to embrace Jesus Christ in faith and in commitment. There is no obvious connection between this event of conversion and the baptism and/or confirmation of the convert. And no preparation for the event was necessary.

As we now turn to examine the teaching and practice of Charles Finney and others of the modern period, we shall note that the instantaneous nature of conversion is much emphasised while the relationship with baptism is either denied or deliberately not mentioned. The third characteristic of the evangelical/evangelistic model, as it emerges in this period, is its lack of theological clarity, with the confusion of passive regeneration and active conversion.

From Charles Grandison Finney (1792– 1875) to William Franklin [Billy] Graham (b. 1918)

As a young man Finney was a nominal Christian. It was when he was learning the nature of law and reading the Law of Moses in preparation for his chosen career as a lawyer that he gained an interest in the Bible. This led on to his search for God and personal salvation. He lived at this time in Adams, New York, and what he came to believe was his experience of regeneration or conversion began – as he characteristically put it – in this way: 'On a

Sabbath evening in the autumn of 1821, I made up my mind that I would settle the question of my soul's salvation at once, that if it were possible I would make my peace with God.' He wanted immediate action but found that he could not settle this weighty matter as quickly as he intended. After much searching from Sunday through to Wednesday he felt compelled on the Wednesday morning to go into the nearby woods to pray.

His record of what happened has become part of American religious folklore. This is how he described his experience in his *Autobiography*.

Finally I found myself verging fast to despair. I said to myself, 'I cannot pray. My heart is dead to God, and will not pray.' I then reproached myself for having promised to give my heart to God before I left the woods. When I came to try, I found I could not give my heart to God. My inward soul hung back, and there was no going out of my heart to God. I began to feel deeply that it was too late; that it must be that I was given up of God and was past hope.

The thought was pressing me of the rashness of my promise, that I would give my heart to God that day or die in the attempt. It seemed to me as if that was binding upon my soul; and yet I was going to break my vow. A great sinking and discouragement came over me, and I felt almost too weak to stand upon my knees.

Just at this moment I again thought I heard some one approach me, and I opened my eyes to see whether it were so. But right there the revelation of my pride of heart, as the great difficulty that stood in the way, was distinctly shown to me. An overwhelming sense of my wickedness in being ashamed to have a human being see me on my knees before God, took such powerful possession of me, that I cried at the top of my voice, and exclaimed that I would not leave that place if all the men on earth and all the devils in hell surrounded me. 'What!' I said, 'such a degraded sinner as I am, on my knees confessing my sins to the great and holy God; and ashamed to have any human being, and a sinner like myself, find me on my knees endeavouring to make my peace with my offended God!' The sin appeared awful, infinite. It broke me down before the Lord.

Just at that point this passage of Scripture seemed to drop into my mind with a flood of light: 'Then shall ye go and pray unto me, and I will hearken unto you. Then shall ye seek me and find me, when ye shall search for me with all your heart.' I instantly seized hold of this with my heart. I had intellectually believed the Bible before; but never had the truth been in my mind that faith was a voluntary trust instead of an intellectual state. I was as conscious as I was of my existence, of trusting at that moment in God's veracity. Somehow I knew that that was a passage of Scripture, though I do not think I had ever read it. I knew that it was God's word, and God's voice, as it were, that spoke to me. I cried to Him, 'Lord, I take thee at thy word. Now thou knowest that I do search for thee with all my heart, and that I have come here to pray to thee; and thou hast promised to hear me.'

That seemed to settle the question that I could then, that day, perform my vow. The Spirit seemed to lay stress upon that idea in the text, 'When you search for me with all your heart.' The question of when, that is of the present time, seemed to fall heavily into my heart. I told the Lord that I should take him at his word; that he could not lie; and that therefore I was sure that he heard my prayer, and that he would be found of me.

He then gave me many other promises, both from the Old and the New Testament, especially some most precious promises respecting our Lord Jesus Christ. I never can, in words, make any human being understand how precious and true those promises appeared to me. I took them one after the other as infallible truth, the assertions of God who could not lie. They did not seem so much to fall into my intellect as into my heart, to be put within the grasp of the voluntary powers of my mind; and I seized hold of them, appropriated them, and fastened upon them with the grasp of a drowning man.

I continued thus to pray, and to receive and appropriate promises for a long time, I know not how long. I prayed till my mind became so full that, before I was aware of it, I was on my feet and tripping up the ascent towards the road. The question of my being converted had not so much as arisen to my thought; but as I went up, brushing through the leaves and bushes, I recollect saying with great emphasis, 'If I am ever converted, I will preach the Gospel.'

His lack of guilt feelings and inner conflict, along with the possession of a quiet mind worried him at this stage. He thought maybe he was not really converted but had driven away the Spirit from his heart.

However, it was not long afterwards that he remained one evening in his office in order to pray. He tells how.

There was no fire, and no light, in the room; nevertheless it appeared to me as if it were perfectly light. As I went in and shut the door after me, it seemed as if I met the Lord Jesus Christ face to face. It did not occur to me then, nor did it for some time afterwards, that it was wholly a mental state. On the contrary it seemed to me that I saw him as I would see any other man. He said nothing, but looked at me in such a manner as to break me right down at his feet. I have always since regarded this as a most remarkable state of mind; for it seemed to me a reality, that he stood before me, and I fell down at his feet and poured out my soul to him. I wept aloud like a child, and made such confessions as I could with my choked utterance. It seemed to me that I bathed his feet with my tears; and yet I had no distinct impression that I touched him, that I recollect.

I must have continued in this state for a good while; but my mind was too much absorbed with the interview to recollect anything that I said. But I know, as soon as my mind became calm enough to break off from the interview, I returned to the front office, and found that the fire that I had made of large wood was nearly burned out. But as I turned and was about to take a seat by the fire, I received a mighty baptism of the Holy Ghost. Without any expectation of it, without ever having the thought in my mind that there was any such thing for me, without any recollection that I had ever heard the thing mentioned by any person in the world, the Holy Spirit descended upon me in a manner that seemed to go through

me, body and soul. I could feel the impression, like a wave of
electricity, going through and through me. Indeed it seemed
to come in waves and waves of liquid love; for I could not
express it in any other way. It seemed like the very breath of
God. I can recollect distinctly that it seemed to fan me, like
immense wings. No words can express the wonderful love
that was shed abroad in my heart. I wept aloud with joy and
love.

So within a very short time Finney had not only been (in
his terms) regenerated and converted, but he had also
received the baptism of the Holy Spirit – an endowment
from on high in order to have power to witness effectively
for Christ. Finney was thus the first of a series of evangelists and missionaries in the nineteenth century who
claimed to have had such an experience and to call it by
this name of 'Baptism in/by/with the Spirit'. Further, we
may observe that though Finney's own path to a sense of
peace with God and power to do his will took several days
of concentrated activity, he came to believe that under
his preaching the whole process could occur in a few
minutes.

When he became a preacher Finney employed the tech-
niques he had witnessed, as well as used, in the courts. He
adapted to the evangelistic task the methods employed by
attorneys as they pleaded their case at the bar. Thus he
pressed for immediate decision, a decision of mind and
will. Further, his reading of the Scriptures and his creation of theology was very much affected by what may be
called legal reasoning. He saw conversion as a decision to
submit to God's moral government; it was an act of the
will, informed by the mind.

He ran into much opposition from his fellow Presby-
terians for his apparent rejection of such basic Reformed
doctrines as the total depravity of the human person
before God, the inability of a sinner to save himself, the
bondage of the will to sin, the absolute need for the inner

working of the Spirit in the soul to create desire for salvation and genuine repentance with faith, and the careful distinction between what God does within the sinner (regeneration) and what the sinner, as enabled by God, does (convert, turn in repentance and faith).

Finney argued in sermons and books that regeneration and conversion are basically identical in meaning and that both terms imply the simultaneous exercise of both human and divine agency. That is, God presents the truth of the Gospel through the Bible or the preacher and in response, by an act of will, the sinner makes himself a new heart (regeneration) or turns to God in repentance and faith (conversion). He is passive in hearing and receiving the Gospel truth; but he is active in acting upon it. So God cannot regenerate or convert a sinner without his full co-operation.

Therefore, in his revival meetings, Finney presented the Gospel to the people as if he were in a court of law arguing the case of one of his clients before judge and jury, and arguing it in order to get the decision he required. Further, to facilitate the process of conversion, Finney began the custom of having people who felt they wanted to convert to sit in special seats at the end of his service for further counselling. Thus began, with these special seats, the custom of evangelists making their appeal to people to come to the front and make their decision for Christ as they did so. Certainly Finney's novel methods seemed to make sense to many Americans in this period of both urbanisation in the East and expansion on the frontier in the West. Further, and this is important, he was by all accounts a holy man, filled with the Holy Spirit, and that Spirit was present in his ministry. Seemingly, his methods and doctrine were hallowed also!

Billy Graham, the best known of modern evangelists, followed in the steps of Finney and all those other evangelists (D. L. Moody, Billy Sunday, R. A. Torrey, etc.)

whose methods were similar to those of Finney. However, his own conversion occurred far away from any evangelistic meeting. He was all alone, feeling abandoned in a love affair, when he decided to submit to the Lord Jesus.

After being an evangelist for the Youth for Christ movement, Graham set up his own organisation, the Billy Graham Evangelistic Association and after the Greater London Crusade in 1954 he became internationally known. All admit that his Crusades are (in the best sense) professionally promoted and organised and that he is a most sincere Christian minister. The climax of all his public, evangelistic meetings is the call for those present who want to make a decision for Christ, or to receive Jesus into their hearts, or to be born again by the Spirit, to stand up in their seats and then to walk down to the front of the auditorium, so that they can be led away for counselling.

A study of his preaching, writing and films reveals that he places great emphasis on the act of deciding for Christ (which he calls by a variety of phrases) immediately, without any delay. There is no doubt that he and all his organisation and helpers are wholly committed to the possibility and reality of instantaneous new birth/conversion, decision for Christ. Here is his own much-repeated direction to people as to how they may immediately become Christians.

> *First*, you must recognize that God loved you so much that He gave His Son to die on the cross. 'For God so loved the world, that he gave his only begotten Son, that whosoever believeth in him should not perish, but have everlasting life' (John 3:16). 'The Son of God . . . loved me, and gave himself for me' (Gal. 2:20).
> *Second*, you must repent of your sins. Jesus said: 'Except ye repent ye shall . . . perish' (Luke 13:3). He said: 'Repent . . . and believe' (Mark 1:15) . . . Repentance does not mean

simply that you are to be sorry for the past. To be sorry is not enough; you must repent. This means that you must turn your back on sins.

Third, you must receive Jesus Christ as Saviour and Lord. 'But as many as received him, to them gave he power to become the sons of God, even to them that believe on his name' (John 1:12). This means that you accept God's offer of love, mercy, and forgiveness. This means that you accept Jesus Christ as your only Lord and your only Saviour. This means that you cease struggling and trying to save yourself. You trust Him completely, without reservation, as your Lord and Saviour.

Fourth, you must confess Christ publicly. Jesus said: 'Whosoever therefore shall confess me before men, him will I confess also before my Father which is in heaven' (Matt. 10:32). This confession carries with it the idea of a life so lived in front of your fellow men that they will see a difference. It means also that you acknowledge with your mouth the Lord Jesus. 'If thou shalt confess with thy mouth the Lord Jesus, and shalt believe in thine heart that God hath raised him from the dead, thou shalt be saved' (Rom. 10:9). It is extremely important that when you receive Christ you tell someone else about it just as soon as possible. This gives you strength and courage to witness.

It is important that you make your decision and your commitment to Christ now. 'Now is the accepted time . . . now is the day of salvation' (II Cor. 6:2). If you are willing to repent of your sins and to receive Jesus Christ as your Saviour, you can do it now. At this moment you can either bow your head or get on your knees and say this little prayer that I have used with thousands of persons on every continent:

O God, I acknowledge that I have sinned against Thee. I am sorry for my sins. I am willing to turn from my sins. I openly receive and acknowledge Jesus Christ as my Saviour. I confess Him as Lord. From this moment on I want to live for Him and serve Him. In Jesus' name, Amen.

If you are willing to make this decision, if you have to the best of your knowledge received Jesus Christ, God's Son, as your own Saviour, then according to the preceding statements of Scripture, you have become a child of God in whom Jesus Christ dwells. Altogether too many people make the mistake of measuring the certainty of their salvation by their feelings. Don't make this serious mistake. Believe God. Take Him at His word.

The kind of direction offered here can be found in much the same form in hundreds of different tracts and booklets produced by modern evangelistic groups.

Following such exhortation or advice, it may be interesting to note the kind of things which are said to those who have come forward in the meeting for counselling. In the Greater London Crusade of 1954 each counsellor was given a leaflet entitled *Lead them to Christ* (published by Team Publications, of London). This is exceptionally well written and presented and, within this form of evangelism, reveals a wisdom not always heard. The first part deals with the character and skills needed by a counsellor who is truly to serve his Lord. The second part is advice on how to deal with the person in the 'Inquiry Room'. Here we learn that 'the inquirer must be allowed to express his need in his own way' and the counsellor must listen carefully. At the appropriate time the counsellor is to make sure that the enquirer knows a minimum of sound Gospel doctrine and is made aware of his genuine need before God of forgiveness and new life. Finally, when the counsellor is convinced that the enquirer really desires to forsake sin and serve the Lord they are 'immediately to kneel down together' and he is 'to lead the soul to Christ as the One who receiveth sinners'. This often involves the enquirer's framing a prayer of confession as provided by Billy Graham in the above quotation. After this the enquirer has become the convert and he is born again. He can now be shown from the Scriptures the many promises that relate to the life of a Christian. 'In this way faith is confirmed by linking his new experience with

the Word of God, showing that every step of the journey
is dependent upon the living Christ.'

Comments

Modern, large-scale evangelism certainly normally seeks
to gain the co-operation of as many congregations as
possible in the area where a Crusade is held. It is from
these churches that workers are recruited to do much of
the preparatory work and then assist in and after the
Crusade. Further, those who 'make a decision' are also
encouraged to return to the church with which they have
a connection or go to the nearest evangelical church.
Follow-up meetings for enquirers/converts are also often
held after the Crusade.

Despite the involvement of the churches, however, this
modern approach to conversion makes no serious attempt
to relate the 'crisis' experience of those who are genuinely
touched by the grace of God to the life of the Church of
God. Take for example the directions given by Billy
Graham and cited above. He calls upon people to confess
Christ, but in the New Testament the primary way of
doing this is by baptism. And baptism tends to be a taboo
subject in Crusades these days – unlike earlier Moody-
Sankey meetings when people were forcibly told that
their baptism and/or confirmation could never save them.
Thus the impression is given that what is important –
indeed of chief importance – is not, as Luther insisted, 'I
have been baptised . . .', but 'I have had an experience I call
conversion . . .' So there is an inbuilt and unexpressed
tendency to devalue the sacraments and the life of the
average congregation.

Further, one cannot but be worried that the meaning
of repentance and faith are given but a minimal and
introductory content in and by this model. This is,

perhaps, inevitable given the circumstances of Crusade-evangelism.

In criticising this evangelistic model of conversion, I want also to remember that, had it not been for the work of evangelists like Billy Graham, the flame of evangelism and the call to turn to God-in-Christ would have become very dim in the Western Church. They are dim now, but they would have been even dimmer. Further, it is salutary to recall that evangelists from Whitefield to Graham came on to the scene and flourished there because the churches, in general, were not themselves involved in that evangelism to which their heavenly, exalted Lord calls them. If the doctrine of conversion is weak in terms of content and application, at least modern evangelists do keep before the whole Church the need always to have the making of disciples/converts high on the agenda.

Finally, a word concerning modern evangelicals who practise believers' baptism. Let us first note the official teaching of the large and influential Southern Baptist Convention of America in its *Statement of Baptist Faith and Message* (1925):

> Christian baptism is the immersion of a believer in water in the name of the Father, and Son and the Holy Spirit. The act is a symbol of our faith in a crucified, buried and risen Saviour. It is prerequisite to the privileges of a church relation and to the Lord's Supper . . .

Earlier in this *Statement* internal regeneration and repentance and faith had been explained in such a manner as to make clear that they have occurred, and that the sinner is forgiven, justified and converted *before* he is actually baptised. Baptism is thus a symbol and sign of something God has already done. In contrast, as we saw in Chapter 5 on the catechumenate model, baptism in the early Church was seen as the event, climax and fulfilment of conversion. Modern Baptists, as far as I know, do not speak of conversion in relation to baptism. Rather, for them, baptism is what follows conversion.

PART 3

MAKING CONVERTS

9

CONVERTEDNESS

The making of converts for Jesus Christ needs to be motivated by the love of Jesus and controlled by a sound doctrine of conversion to God. We have seen that the authentic elements or strands of conversion are conviction of sin, repentance, faith, baptism. In using the words 'strands' and 'elements' I have followed the suggestion of Paul Helm in his *The Beginnings: Word and Spirit in Conversion* (1986). He rejects the word 'stages' as implying that there is a logical or experimental progression through conviction, repentance and faith. In reality, as we have seen, they both overlap and mix into each other. Like Helm, we have also insisted that there are two sides to the coin we call conversion: there is the divine side via the Word and the Spirit and there is the human response via repentance and faith.

But, in the light of the undoubted success of the evangelistic model must we include baptism (with incorporation into church fellowship) as an element of conversion? Does not doing so not only exclude the vast membership of the Salvation Army but also many other fine, holy Christians who place little or no value on baptism? Will the unbaptised or those who effectively deny their baptism by saying it is unimportant be excluded from the kingdom of God of the age to come?

What we have to say is that it is God who has revealed to us the elements or strands of conversion. They are his requirements addressed to those in whose hearts, minds and wills the Holy Spirit is working. While it is our duty to fulfil those requirements, it is his right and prerogative to cancel one or more of them in terms of his conditions for entry into the kingdom of God and the blessings of eternal life. It would seem to be the case that, because of the way the Church has failed to administer holy baptism, God has made it possible for people to enter into union with himself through Jesus without baptism. To say this does not allow us also to say that we should neglect baptism. It is to say that God is kind and good and sometimes chooses to bless us, despite our failures!

What was important in the Church in New Testament times and has always been paramount is that church members be truly in a state of convertedness. The event of conversion – however it occurs – is decisive, but it must be followed by a life of commitment, dedication and devotion to Jesus Christ. Each of us needs to ask whether or not we are conscious of our sins, trusting in the grace of God revealed in Jesus, following in the way taught by our Lord, and seeking to serve him in the fellowship of the people of God (Church) and in his world.

Convertedness and imperfection

A lot of people who sincerely believe themselves to be Christians and genuinely want to be committed Christians are worried because they seem to be achieving more failure than success. Here are some principles to help you, if you or others you know, are in this state.

1. Convertedness does not mean that you are holy through and through

Jesus himself was truly holy, for he was wholly consecrated to the service of the heavenly Father. He faced strong temptations to think and act in ways contrary to the will of God, but he resisted them and always faithfully obeyed the heavenly requirement. However, he did not possess, as we do, a sinful human nature. His human nature was without any inherent bias towards evil and thus, though he faced powerful testing and temptation, he did not have the same inner battle as we do. This is not to say that his temptations were less than ours: as Messiah he faced extraordinarily powerful testing and temptation. Rather, it is to say that Christians within whom is the seed of eternal life and the presence of the Holy Spirit have not only to resist temptations from without but also to overcome evil impulses from within. Until you die you will have your present human nature and body and thus the ever-present possibility of sinful thoughts and intentions arising within your heart.

The Christian life is always a battle against the world, the flesh (sinful human nature) and the devil (Satan). Holiness is being conformed to the will of God, not the accepted standards of secular society: it is overcoming evil and sinful impulses and thoughts and thinking pure, wholesome and true thoughts; and it is resisting the temptations of the devil to act contrary to the known will of God. It is because holiness is always a goal to aim for that the New Testament contains many exhortations to disciples of Jesus to set that goal before you. Here are several of these exhortations: 'Be perfect, therefore, as your heavenly Father is perfect' (Matt. 5:48); 'Be holy, because I am holy' (1 Pet. 1:16); and 'Be imitators of God . . . and be [continually] filled with the Spirit' (Eph. 5:1, 18).

The real point is not 'are you holy now?'; but, 'are you desirous from the bottom of your heart to be wholly

consecrated to the service of Christ and the will of God?'
Are you wanting and trying to live as a baptised believer who
in Christ has already died to sin and been raised to new life
and hope? Do you recognise your failures and weaknesses
and confess them with a penitent heart to your heavenly
Father, asking for his forgiveness? Convertedness means
that you desire to be holy and want God to make you holy.

2. Convertedness does not mean that your life as a professing Christian will always be smooth and without accident, tragedy and problems

Jesus himself was not exempt from pain, suffering and
horrible death. The apostles also faced all kinds of difficulties from persecution to shipwreck and from hunger to
imprisonment (2 Cor. 6:3ff.). We do not know *why* this or
that happens to us: you do not know why you develop
cancer, why you were in a major accident, why you were
made bankrupt, why you lost a loved one in tragic circumstances, or why you were made redundant. We live in a
world which has much sorrow, pain and distress and, as a
Christian believer, you are not exempt from these things.
Further, as a Christian, it is possible that God may ask you
to suffer for your commitment to Jesus Christ. Thus, on top
of the problems and difficulties that come your way as a
human being living in human society, you may also face
further pain because you identify with Jesus Christ. Thousands of Christians have faced persecution joyfully because
they bear the name of Jesus.

If convertedness does not exempt you from suffering it
does mean, however, that you have the potentiality of
facing the suffering in a noble and dignified way. Because
you are following Jesus, who suffered, you have the
supreme example to follow. Further, you have a multitude
of promises within the books of the New Testament
promising special help and succour to those who suffer as

Christians (e.g. Romans 8:22ff.; 1 Peter 1:3ff.). To suffer nobly, and as Christ suffered, is not easy; but as a Christian you face problems, hardships and difficulties knowing that your heavenly Father knows all about your condition, and that the Holy Spirit within you is there to strengthen and help you. God's will is always to cause you to grow in wisdom and love through such experiences even if you cannot, either within them or after them, see *why* they occurred.

3. Convertedness does not mean that, of necessity, you enjoy the distinct, inner testimony of the Holy Spirit

Writing to the Romans, Paul spoke of a special, inner conviction of being a child of God – a conviction caused directly by the Holy Spirit himself. After insisting that the Spirit dwells in the hearts of all genuine believers (8:9ff.) so that with his prompting each believer may truly address God as 'dear Father', he adds this significant information. 'The Spirit himself testifies with our spirit that we are God's children' (v. 16).

Such testimony is over and above self-consciousness and the inner sense of belonging to God through Christ by the Spirit. It is a distinct, special testimony and witness that is probably to be equated with what is elsewhere called 'the seal' of the Spirit (2 Cor. 1:22; Eph. 1:13; 4:30; John 6:27). Some Christians are certainly given this inner testimony and by it they know, without a shadow of doubt, that God is truly there, that Christ is their Lord and Saviour and that they are safely in his care and keeping. Other Christians seem not to have it, for they are plagued with doubt and uncertainty as to whether or not they really and truly belong to God-in-Christ.

Not a few books have been written, sermons preached and talks given in order to explain to Christians that, while this special testimony of the Spirit is part of God's full provision for believers, it is not a necessary part of being a Christian. Some believers seem to have this wonderful assurance from their first believing while others gain it later. It seems to be especially evident in times of revival and renewal of the Church, and those who possess it usually have a great desire to witness for their Lord and Saviour, telling others of what he offers them in his great and everlasting salvation. Yet it is a gift for which we ought to long and pray.

4. *Convertedness does not necessarily mean that you are baptised with the Holy Spirit and exercise one or more of the special gifts of the Spirit*

The apostle Paul made it clear that it is only by the inspiration of the Spirit that a repenting person can truly confess that Jesus is Lord (1 Cor. 12:3). Further he taught that by the action of the Spirit, that is by the personal agency of the Spirit, you are placed in the body of Christ: the Spirit as the baptiser actually introduces you to, and places you within, the body of Christ (1 Cor. 12:13). And he held that the Christian is a person in whom the Spirit actually dwells (Rom. 8:9–11). Therefore, convertedness means that the Spirit of God dwells in your heart whether or not you 'feel' his presence and power.

It has been the experience of many Christians, from the time of the apostles to the present, that God actually seems to pour out his Spirit upon them. This experience has been called 'baptism with the Spirit' and 'being filled with the Spirit' and it is felt as a divine visitation from outside coming upon and entering in. There are several descriptions of this experience in the Acts of the Apostles (2:4ff.; 8:14–18; 10:45, etc.) which Luke appears to understand as fulfilments of the promise made by John the Baptist. He said of Jesus that 'he . . . will baptise with the Holy Spirit' (John 1:33). Accompanying the heavenly visitation, as recorded by Luke, were all kinds of phenomena – not only speaking in tongues but also physical events like the shaking of a house.

In times of revival and renewal Christians have believed that the powerful, spiritual experiences they enjoyed were nothing less than visitations by the Holy Spirit. And the most common result of such experiences has been that the recipients have felt an overwhelming love for God (Rom. 5:5, 'God has poured out his love into our hearts') and a desire to tell others of that love (see no. 3 above). In the modern Pentecostal and Charismatic movements, too, much was made, especially in the early days, of speaking in tongues as being the universal proof of the baptism with the Spirit. This teaching was a mistake, for when the Spirit descends upon a believer, the gifts he brings are in the royal bounty of Christ, the Lord, and vary from person to person, as also does the nature of the ways the visitation of the Spirit is felt and known.

This heavenly baptism with the Spirit is repeatable and is not a once-for-all event. Christ the Lord is able to send the Spirit wherever and whenever he will. And he sends him to penitent, humble and seeking people, often unexpectedly.

Therefore, while it is true that each Christian is indwelt by the Holy Spirit, it is also true that from time to time, here and there, the exalted Lord Jesus Christ pours out the Spirit *upon* Christians in order to make them more effective as his disciples, messengers and ambassadors in this world. It would seem that when the Church of God is functioning within the will and purpose of God it is a people who are baptised with the Spirit. It would seem also that the Letters within the New Testament were written by their apostolic authors on the supposition that the local churches knew experientially the baptism with the Holy Spirit (e.g., Gal. 3:5; 5:13ff.). Today, the norm of the churches in the West does not appear to be 'being filled with the Spirit': this is regrettable but it does not mean that the churches are not composed of converted souls!

5. Convertedness does not mean, of necessity, that you know the contents of the Bible well and are proficient in prayer and meditation

You may have heard the Gospel, received and believed it, without actually reading the Bible. Before the invention of printing, thousands of Christians never read the Bible: they heard it read and taught and committed to memory as much as they were able. It takes a long time to master the basic contents of the New Testament, let alone the Old Testament. What matters is not so much whether you have read and understood, but whether or not you have a sincere desire to read, study, learn and inwardly digest the contents of the Scriptures. As one old prayer expresses it: 'Blessed Lord, who hast caused all holy Scriptures to be written for our learning; grant that we may in such wise hear them, read, mark, learn and inwardly digest them, that by patience, and comfort of thy holy Word, we may embrace and ever hold fast the blessed hope of everlasting life, which thou hast given us in our Saviour, Jesus Christ.'

There is a sense in which a converted soul must pray for 'prayer is the soul's sincere desire, uttered or unexpressed'. However, desire and commitment have to be complemented by discipline and method both in prayer and in meditation. Prayer includes adoration, praise, thanksgiving, confession of sins, intercession for others and petitions for self. Meditation involves a technique and has to be learned by determination as well as trial and error. It is one of the ways God has designed to help his children take the truth and grace of God from their minds to their hearts and into action. (See further my recent book, *Longing for the Heavenly Realm*, which has several chapters on contemplation/meditation.)

6. Convertedness is certainly to be turned, in discipleship of Jesus, towards the God and Father of our Lord Jesus Christ, being attracted by him and longing to enter fully into his presence in the heavenly kingdom

In union with Jesus through the Holy Spirit, a disciple is enjoying *already* God's salvation in terms of forgiveness and the gift of eternal life. However, that for which the disciple longs is *not yet* available, for the fullness of communion, fellowship, joy and peace will be a reality only in the sphere where Christ is and will be. Convertedness is not a static situation and experience: it is like being within the magnetic field of a magnet of love as you are drawn into deeper experience of the love of God. It is movement towards the vision of God through growing, following, learning, obeying, trusting and sojourning. Further, it is not an individual journey and pilgrimage, for it is made with others who are heading for the same destination. It is a walking together, led by the Spirit, in faith, hope and love. There will be stumbling and losing of the way; there will be retreat as well as advance; there will be the rough and the smooth; and there will be pain and disappointment. Yet the pure in heart shall see God and this vision of God in his absolute perfection and purity will, through Christ and by the Holy Spirit, draw believers towards itself via that last enemy, death itself.

Conversion to God consists, as we have seen, in conviction of sin, repentance, faith, baptism and incorporation into the living Church. Convertedness does not cancel these elements, but consists of them and other elements – e.g. faithfulness, hope, love, joy and peace. The Christian life always includes conviction of sin, repentance for sin, turning to God in faith, obeying the will of God and looking to him for salvation. The big difference in these elements before and after conversion is that they are offered to God from a different status. In the original turning to God in conversion, repentance and faith are offered as from a lost orphan, longing to be saved and placed within the family of God; the repentance and faith of the converted person are offered as from an adopted child in the family, who already knows experientially the love of God.

10

REGAINING THE VISION

We face a situation in the West wherein major churches/
denominations are losing membership and becoming peri-
pheral to, and marginalised in, the society they seek to
serve. In order to become 'relevant' and to be seen to be
useful, ecclesiastical leaders, at both national and local level,
apparently feel that they need to address contemporary
social, political and economic matters, making 'Christian'
comment in sermons or by way of a resolution in synod.
And as they address these issues they have less and less to say
about what may be called the individual's relationship to
God-in-Christ and the need of society for the good news of
salvation from sin and into the kingdom of God (of the age
to come).

Therefore, it is not surprising that the Churches (at least
on the evidence of official pronouncements) have moved so
far from the state of being normally committed to making
converts to Christ that such expressions as 'conversion',
'new birth' and 'deciding for Christ' are seen as the special
vocabulary of the enthusiasts – the 'born again' crowd or the
'Charismatics'. Occasionally, as much to show their wide
sympathies as anything else, denominational leaders will
appear on the same platform as leading evangelists such as
Billy Graham; though lip-service, and maybe occasional

involvement, are made to evangelistic enterprises, however, the general state of affairs within the churches is
neither conducive to, nor expectant of, numerical growth
through conversions. And this is true whether we think of
conversion as the return to full Christian commitment of
those who were baptised as babies and have left the congregation, or as the bringing into the Christian fellowship of
those who never had a place in it.

Needing revival

Various reasons may be offered for this strange state of
affairs wherein a diminishing Church is preaching a basically this-worldly salvation to fewer people. We can adduce
the failure of the Church, the increasingly secularist nature
of Western society, and the absence of the presence and
power of the Holy Spirit. And, when we reflect upon these
three, we realise that they are interrelated. The secularisation of Western society has gone on apace, in part because
of the spiritual weakness of the Church, which has been
unsure of the presence of the power of the Holy Spirit. And,
when in motion, the secularist spirit has been harmful to the
search for the realm of the Spirit. So much so that salvation
can now be presented wholly in this-worldly terms by those
who claim to be religious teachers and leaders.

Secularisation may be defined in various ways. First of all,
it may point to the obvious way in which various social
institutions have been removed from either specifically
ecclesiastical or general religious control. Here we may
think of schools, colleges, universities, along with social
welfare agencies. Christianity/religion is seen as that which
is the preserve of the Church. Thus the Church and her faith
is one part of a complex society. Then, in the second place, it
may point to the way in which religious imagery, symbolism and rituals become less common and influential in

society (e.g. christenings, church weddings and funerals) and at the same time Christian interpretations of life, death and morality become less well known and passed on. Thus to practise religion becomes a private option, open to those who incline to that way of believing and living within the pluralist society. In an extreme form, this development leaves people – at least the majority – unable to make sense of talk of divine revelation, the supernatural, the Holy Trinity and so on.

It is certainly true that among younger people there is much less knowledge of the contents of the Bible and of classic Christian literature today than there was a century ago. This means that effective and genuine Christian evangelism has first of all to provide basic teaching about God as Creator and judge, before it can specifically present the good news concerning Jesus Christ and make the call to repentance and faith. Further, since religious education in schools often is now no more than the provision of minimal information about the religions of the whole world, along with selective material on differing systems of morality, evangelism has also to justify both the exclusive uniqueness of Christ as Incarnate Son of God and of Christian morality as flowing from commitment to him.

The evangelist who holds that all religions are ways to God's salvation or that sincere religious people of all types are baptised into Christ with a baptism of sincerity (even though they do not know this to be the case!) will hardly have a compelling conviction to proclaim the good news. Unless he truly holds that turning to the God and Father of the Lord Jesus Christ brings salvation qualitatively different from that found in the practice of Judaism, Islam and other religions, and unless he believes that decent, affluent 'half-believers in their casual creeds' are called by God to repentance and faith, then his job specification will need totally rewriting.

If I were asked to isolate one reason for the general lack of confidence in the Gospel of God and the power of the Holy Spirit to make the Gospel effective, it would be that we have not had a major revival in the West for a very long time. Where there is an outpouring of the Spirit, there is no failure of nerve within the Church with respect to the Gospel. Let us be clear. The desire to evangelise, the desire to make converts and the desire to see the body of Christ grow in holiness and commitment to mission is a God-given desire. It is strongest, and more quickly turns into effective action, when people are filled with the Holy Spirit.

In a revival the congregations of Christians are quite sure that God is the *living* Lord, that their sins are offensive to him, that Christ died for their sins and rose for their forgiveness and justification, and that, in and through Christ, God offers and gives them pardon of sin and his Holy Spirit to indwell them. When a Christian is filled with the Spirit he/she looks upon other people in the love of Christ and sees them as needing God's grace, as potential members of the family and household of God. He/she cares not whether the person is of this or that persuasion for his/her great care is that this person is encountered by Christ.

We have not had the Spirit of God visiting our churches as a mighty wind: true, in such movements as the Charismatic movement, we have sensed his presence and power as that of a gentle breeze and the results have been many – from the renewal of whole congregations through healing of the sick to individual conversions. However, if the Church at large, in the context of the increasing secularisation of society and pluralism within it, is to recover its nerve and vision for the Gospel then only a revival will suffice. I fully recognise that such a divine event is controlled from heaven not earth and to state the need does not bring the event into being.

There would seem to be some kind of correlation between the sincere desiring, longing and yearning of the faithful people of God on earth and the response from heaven. And revival when it comes begins in the churches but quickly sends forth the renewed people in God with the Gospel into the world around them. To say this is not to say that the Church should sit back and wait for revival: of course the people of God are to act as the people of God now, praying for strength to do so and expressing the deep longing for greater manifestations of the divine presence and power.

It is perhaps appropriate at this point to provide a sketch of the type of heavenly confidence that a church needs to be a centre for evangelism, that is evangelism as a constant commitment and activity within the context of its worship, fellowship and service. Evangelism is at the very centre of the mission of the Church in society: evangelism is the very core of that which the Church does as she crosses the frontiers into the world. It is not the proclamation in an objective way of a series of truths concerning God and Jesus and salvation. It is proclamation of God's saving action in Jesus Christ by people who are involved with those whom they wish to hear, receive and obey the Gospel.

Those who actually bear the Gospel and witness to and for Jesus Christ are essentially related to the message they present: its effects are to be seen in their lives and relationship to their hearers. In this sense true evangelism is incarnational, being proclamation and teaching along with involvement with and commitment to people, wherever they may be. True evangelism can never merely be the quick visit to declare the Gospel and then the hasty retreat into the safety of home or church building.

Confidence

Fundamental to genuine confidence is *confidence in God as the living, reigning, loving and active Lord.* This is a deep inner conviction that God truly exists and is in dynamic and gracious contact with his people in his world. In its profoundest sense this confidence is the experience of the Spirit testifying with our spirits that we are God's children, creating within us a joy that is beyond description.

All who read the eighth chapter of Paul's Letter to the Romans must be impressed with his humble yet unbounded confidence in God. After expressing his confidence in God's providence in daily life (8:28), he moves on to express his confidence in the eternal, electing love of God in Christ and of the eternal validity of the saving action of God in the death, resurrection and exaltation of Jesus. With such a God, he cries out, what have we to fear or to want? And he concludes: 'I am convinced that neither death nor life, neither angels nor demons, neither the present nor the future, nor any powers, neither height nor depth, nor anything else in all creation, will be able to separate us from the love of God that is in Christ Jesus our Lord' (8:37–9).

It is probably true to say that many sincere Christians do believe in God as the sacred Scriptures present him, but they lack any real, unmistakable sense of his power and glory. They do not have that witness of the Holy Spirit with their hearts that God is truly and really their heavenly Father. And, of course, the kind of view of the natural world that we pick up from popular science – in school or on TV – does not help us to have sensitivity to the realm of the supernatural, above, beyond and through the natural world. But when the Spirit of God comes upon a group of people they know in their hearts beyond all doubt that God is everything that the New Testament tells us he is. They become humbly confident in him and everything he has revealed and said.

Arising from experience of the living God and, at the same time, feeding into that experience, is *confidence in the Scriptures as trustworthy records of what God wants people to know and to receive.* As a collection of documents from different centuries, the Bible is a fascinating book, and, as such, provides interesting reading and study material. But the person who has confidence in God and in his self-revelation recorded in Scripture can never be content with such study. He or she will read the Bible on bended knee – that is, in a state of humble receptivity and expectancy – waiting for a word from the Lord, for an insight into his will, and for a warming of the heart. He or she will listen to the public reading of the Bible and its exposition within worship as a further opportunity to learn from heaven. And because of this confidence in the Bible as the book of revelation and of the Holy Spirit he or she receives as true what is taught therein concerning the nature and the destiny of mankind.

He or she accepts that human beings are created by God to enjoy him and all his blessings while also devoting their whole lives to glorifying their Creator. He or she accepts that there is something fundamentally wrong with the position of mankind before God and because of this mankind needs to be redeemed, restored to what God originally planned, and so blessed as never again to fall into the delusion of sin. And he or she accepts that to redeem, restore and save mankind God took the costly step of becoming incarnate as Jesus of Nazareth and as the man for others doing for mankind what it could not do for itself by his life, teaching, example and compassion, and particularly by his sacrificial, atoning death and glorious resurrection and ascension. So he or she wholeheartedly believes that Jesus Christ, the man for others, is the one in, by and through whom we come to God and receive salvation.

In the contemporary Church there are so many hindrances to possession of a confidence in the Scriptures as the faithful record of God's will and words. So much study of the Scriptures is dominated by the 'critical' methods used in the study of ancient literature that Christian people appear never to have been taught (or to have perhaps lost) the habit of reading and hearing the Bible as living words from God in heaven. In fact, to state it in this way would invite criticism from the majority of clergy and church leaders. Yet in times of revival when the Spirit of the Lord falls upon the people who are believers, such people adopt or revert to a simple (a profoundly simple) approach to the Bible. They do not read it looking for problems and inconsistencies, for pre-modern views of mankind and of the divine character, and for ancient, out-of-date concepts of salvation and redemption.

Rather, they read it humbly, eagerly, expectantly and faithfully as children wanting to hear from their Father, as beggars wanting to be fed, and as soldiers waiting for their marching orders. Of course there is a place for biblical scholarship of a reverent and believing kind: of course there is a place for careful exegesis and interpretation of the contents of the various books of the Bible. These activities ought to go alongside the reading, studying and meditating upon the Scriptures in the manner in which we have been describing. But the usual methods of biblical scholarship employed in the secular university will never, if brought into the Church directly and without adaptation, create a sense of confidence in the Scriptures as the faithful words of God.

Confidence in God and in his Word naturally leads to *confidence in his mission to his world, into which he invites the Church to enter*. God sent forth his Son into the world in order to save the world. The Son, having done all that was necessary to save the world, returned in his humanity to heaven and sent the Holy Spirit to empower and guide his disciples in their involvement in God's mission in the world. This mission is to create in and by Jesus Christ (the exalted, Incarnate Son of God) a new people to become the people of the new cosmos (new heaven and earth) of the kingdom of God of the age to come. The Church is intended to be the fellowship of people in whom God has created the beginnings of the new life of the kingdom of God, and that, as such, it is to be a society of men and women who share what they have been given and witness to the love and grace of God.

When the Spirit of God is poured out upon the Church, the society of Christians are sure that they belong primarily to the heavenly realm where Christ is enthroned as Lord at the right hand of the Father, and that in union with him they sit there with him. Thus they set their minds on this heavenly realm and being identified with the exalted Christ seek to see the world through his eyes and with his love. They see their calling on earth as bearing witness in attitude, word and deed to the one to whom they belong and the new creation arising around him in the heavenly realm. In fellowship and worship they celebrate their union with Christ and the salvation into which they have entered; in proclaiming and teaching the good news of the resurrected and exalted Lord Jesus they invite people to enter the new creation and by particular concern for the poor, outcasts and needy they testify to the love that is supreme in the kingdom of God.

When the Church loses its confidence in its union with the exalted Lord Jesus and the longing for that heavenly realm becomes weak or extinct, then the sense of involvement in God's mission takes a different emphasis. Celebration is of the good things in this world only and mission is improving the lot of people in this world with a vague sense that God plans to bring in the kingdom into the present world and age. The sense of being a pilgrim people who are sojourners in this world and who have set their hearts upon the realm where Christ is, is lost and the emphasis is upon the Church as the servant – serving the perceived needs of society from the perspective of love of the neighbour for this world and age. And confidence is placed in political and social change.

Confidence in God as Lord, his revealed Word and will and in his mission in his world leads to *confidence in the Christ who is the centre of the proclamation and teaching*. The New Testament and the Church over the centuries clearly teach that Jesus is unique. He is so, not only because he is perfect man but also because he is the eternal Son of God made man. In confessing that he is truly God and truly man, that is God become man, Christians are expressing a truth that they cannot wholly understand, but which they believe to be the case. They recognise that all the claims they make about his identity and his achievement on behalf of mankind have their origin in the fact of Incarnation. Were he not the Incarnate God, how could he be the true and only mediator between God and mankind? As man he brings mankind to God and as God he brings God to mankind. Having offered himself as a sacrificial atonement for the sins of the world and having overcome death, he is as God-made-man able to unite deity and humanity for everlasting salvation.

So salvation is only in union with Jesus, who is the way, truth and the life, for no one comes to the Father except in and through him. With this estimate of Jesus, the Church is impelled to proclaim the good news to the world, for the world is seen as in need of him and he is seen as more than ready to meet the true and real need of the world. When the Holy Spirit comes upon a society of Christians, they see very clearly that they (and all mankind) are sinners and that Jesus is the perfect Saviour, who is ever ready to enter into communion with those who receive him.

When the Church looks at Jesus through the spectacles provided by a secularist culture, then he becomes a Saviour acceptable to the modern mind. His virginal conception and bodily resurrection are explained in such a way as to lose their literal, physical meaning: appearances of Jesus to the disciples are explained as objective or subjective visions and the exaltation into heaven is taken as a myth based on the idea of a three-tier universe. He emerges as an interesting, perhaps fascinating, person who is an important symbol of all that is good and noble in this world and whose life and words give us important clues as to what the invisible God is like. However, he is not the person whose deity is so clearly affirmed in the Catholic creeds and in the historic, traditional liturgies. He is hardly the kind of person in whose name a mission to the world would be mounted.

So it is not surprising that as the commitment to the orthodox doctrine of Jesus as God-made-man has weakened within theological scholarship and ecclesiastical leadership, so views of other religions (in the context of a shrinking world in a jet age) have also changed. While the Church once said that Christ is the exclusive Saviour – in him alone is the only pathway to God – voices within are now saying loudly and clearly that if Jesus is Saviour it is in an inclusive sense. By such a claim is meant that sincere people in all religions are groping after truth and Jesus is truth: thus all religions can be ways to God's salvation. Of course the concept of Jesus as an inclusive Saviour comes in a variety of forms and there is talk of 'inclusivism from above' and 'from below'; but all forms see Christ as the apex of the triangle. Though this approach preserves to a certain extent the uniqueness of Jesus it does so by taking away the urgency and need for evangelisation by the Church of God. Rather it encourages serious dialogue and co-operation only.

The development of inclusivist doctrines of the uniqueness of Jesus are now, however, under criticism within the Church because they are said to be essentially paternalistic or colonialist. The commitment to tolerance/toleration has the effect, in these circumstances, of causing Christians to adopt pluralism in the sense of seeing Christ as one, but by no means the only one, of the ways/persons who reveal God to us and give us a pattern of life to follow. When we get to this stage then evangelism is a word for the archives, not for contemporary vocabulary! When a Church is filled with the Holy Spirit in a time of revival it tends towards an exclusivist view of Christ, but does so without in any way denying the dignity of all mankind, made in the image and likeness of God.

No doubt there are many possible ways of describing the nature of the major religions of the world and their relationship to Christ: no doubt also the relationship posited between Judaism and Christ will not be the same as that between Hinduism or Islam and Christ. This said, where the Church is filled with the Spirit and holds to the received,

orthodox view of Jesus as the Incarnate Son of God then it
will have confidence in the proclamation of him as the sole
mediator between God and mankind.

In this world but not of it

We have looked at confidence in God as Lord, in the
Scriptures, in the mission of God and in Christ as the centre
of the Gospel: we could, of course, add to these and speak of
confidence in the promises that tell of life after death with
Christ in God's new heaven and earth and in those that
speak of God's ultimate control of history and human
destiny. However, enough has been written to indicate the
type of humble and spiritual confidence produced in
Christians when they are filled with the Spirit – which is the
'normal' state in which God wishes his Church to be. In
reading this account some will probably express fear that
such confidence as has been described causes people to have
a debased view of this world and not to see the genuine good
and joy within it as God's creation. To help those with such
fears here are some thoughts from Dr E. L. Mascall:

> What is our attitude to this world to be? Treat it as if it is all that
> there is and as if all that you need is to be found in it, and it will
> dangle its gifts before your eyes, decoy you, tantalize you, and
> finally mock and desert you, leaving you empty handed and
> with ashes in your mouth.
>
> But treat it as the creation of God, as truly good because it is
> God's handiwork and yet not the highest good because it is not
> God himself, live in this world as one who knows that the world
> is God's and yet as one who knows that his true home is not here
> but in eternity, and the world itself will yield up to you joys
> and splendours of whose very existence the mere worldling is
> utterly ignorant. Then you will see the world's transience and
> fragility, its finitude and its powerlessness to satisfy, not as signs
> that life is a bad joke with man as the helpless victim, but as pale

and splintered reflections of the splendour and beauty of the eternal God – that beauty ever old and ever new – in whom alone man can find lasting peace and joy.

It has been a surprise to many who have experienced conversion to God in Christ that they have not only perceived the grace of God in Jesus Christ but also seen God revealed in and through nature. The grass has become greener, the skies bluer and the whole world of nature more welcoming and full of blessings. Yet this world only offers partial, broken and fleeting glimpses of perfection which come and go, wither and die: perfection that lasts and satisfies is to be found only in union with God through Jesus Christ in everlasting love in heaven. Conversion is a turning from seeing this world in categories within this world to a seeing of this world in the light of that other supernatural world where Christ is enthroned as Lord.

Appendix 1

CONVERSION IN THE OLD TESTAMENT

In the Greek translation (Septuagint) of the Hebrew Bible (our Old Testament) the verb *epistrephein* (along with *apostrephein*) translates the Hebrew verb, *Shubh*, in the places where the latter has a specifically theological meaning of converting to, turning to or returning to God.

In all the verb *Shubh* occurs around 1,050 times in the Hebrew Bible and in most cases the meaning is that of literal and physical turning. However, in around 120 cases the meaning is theological, indicating a different attitude towards God and a new pattern of behaviour. It is thus used in the religious sense to point to the return to the covenant relationship that God originally brought into being between himself and the people of Israel. That relationship was one which required worship, trust, love and obedience with a rejection of all other forms of religion.

Here are some examples of the use of *Shubh* in this theological sense:

1. 2 Chronicles 30:6–9. The revival of pure religion under King Hezekiah, who sent out this letter to his people:

People of Israel, *return* to the LORD, the God of Abraham, Isaac and Israel, that he may return to you who are left, who have escaped from the hand of the kings of Assyria ...

If you *return* to the LORD, then your brothers and your

children will be shown compassion by their captors and
will come back to this land, for the LORD your God is
gracious and compassionate. He will not turn his face
from you if you *return* to him.

2. Isaiah 55:5–7. A call to the Jewish exiles.

Seek the LORD while he may be found; call upon him while
he is near. Let the wicked forsake his way and the evil man
his thoughts. Let him *turn* to the LORD, and he will have
mercy on him, and to our God, for he will freely pardon.

3. Ezekiel 18:21–3. A message to the individual Jew.

But if a wicked man *turns away* from all the sins he has
committed and keeps all my decrees and does what is just
and right, he will surely live; he will not die . . . Do I take
any pleasure in the death of the wicked? declares the
Sovereign LORD. Rather, am I not pleased when they *turn*
from their ways and live?

4. Joel 2:12–13. Israel ought to repent.

'Even now,' declares the LORD, '*return* to me with all your
heart, with fasting and weeping and mourning.'

Rend your heart and not your garments. *Return* to the
LORD your God, for he is gracious and compassionate,
slow to anger and abounding in love, and he relents from
sending calamity.

5. Psalm 80:3, 7, 19. Only with God's help can Israel return
to him. He must restore (cause to turn).

Restore us, O God Almighty; make your face shine upon
us, that we may be saved.

Therefore it may be seen how Jesus, following John the
Baptist, took up this prophetic call to God's covenant
people to 'turn/return/be restored'. The verb which is used
in the Gospels and Acts to convey the idea of turning from
sin is *metanoiein* usually translated as 'to repent'. This verb is
not, however, used in the Septuagint to translate *Shubh*. So,
while it is in the message of John the Baptist, Jesus and his
apostles the dynamic equivalent of *Shubh*, it is not so in the
Greek Old Testament for there the verb *epistrephein* has that

function. But for *metanoiein* to gain the full meaning of *Shubh*, and thus of *epistrephein*, it is complemented by the verb *pisteuein*, to believe. Jesus preached, 'Repent and believe . . .' which is the same as 'Turn/return/convert . . .'

Commenting on the verb *Shubh* in its religious/theological usage, Professor Walter Eichrodt wrote:

The metaphor [of turning] was an especially suitable one, for not only did it describe the required behaviour as a real act – 'to make a turn' – and so preserve the strong, personal impact; it also included both the negative element of turning away from the direction taken hitherto and the positive element of turning towards, and so, when combined with prepositions, allowed the rich content of all the many other idioms to be reproduced tersely yet unmistakably (*Theology of the O.T.*, vol. 2, London, S.C.M. Press, 1967, pp. 465–6).

Appendix 2

THE CONTEXT OF 'TO CONVERT'

In the New Testament we are faced with a variety of verbs setting forth (a) human duty to God because of his Gospel, and (b) that which God, in grace, does for sinners responding to his Gospel. These verbs often overlap in meaning even though each has its own particular emphasis. The word 'conversion' can be used as an umbrella kind of term to cover the result of all that is indicated by these verbs. Such usage is, however, not to be recommended! In the lists below the most common English form of the verb is given, followed by the Greek original. Full references to texts are not supplied for the reader can find them all by the use of a Concordance to either the NIV or the RSV (or the use of *The New Strong's Exhaustive Concordance of the Bible*).

1. *What God requires of a person who hears the Gospel:* He or she is,
   (a) To believe it (*pisteuein*); Acts 2:44; 4:4; 4:32.
   (b) To repent of sin (*metanoiein*); Acts 2:38; 3:19; 8:22.
   (c) To obey it (*hypakouein*); Rom. 6:16; Heb. 5:9; 2 Thess. 1:8.
   (d) To receive it (*lambanein*); John 1:12, 16; 5:43; 13:20.
   (e) To convert to God (*epistrephein*); Acts 9:35; 11:21; 26:18.

(f) To confess Christ (*homologein*); Rom. 10:9–10; 1 John 2:23; 4:15.

2. *What God does for a person who receives the Gospel:*
   (a) He (effectually) calls him (*kalein*); Mark 1:20; Rom. 8:30; 9:24; 1 Cor. 1:9.
   (b) He begets new life in him (*gennan*); John 3:3, 5, 6; 1 John 2:29; 3:9.
   (c) He forgives/pardons him (*aphienai*); Mark 2:5; 1 John 1:9; Jas. 5:15.
   (d) He justifies him (*dikaioun*); Luke 18:14; Rom. 3:24, 26; 5:1; 8:33.
   (e) He sanctifies him (*hagiazein*); John 17:17; Acts 20:32; 1 Cor. 1:2.
   (f) He adopts him as his child (*lambanein huiothesia*); Rom. 8:15; Gal. 4:5.
   (g) He baptises him in water and in the Spirit (*baptizein*); Mark 1:8; Acts 1:5; 11:16; Gal. 3:27.

It is a mistake to try to put either what the sinner ought to do or what God graciously does into some kind of chronological – or even logical – order. A person does not simply repent and then having repented believe: the two movements of heart, mind and will are fused and occur simultaneously. Likewise, God's actions are both within the individual and within (as it were) the court of heaven for as he regenerates he also declares a person to be accounted righteous for Christ's sake (to justify). Further, to sanctify implies both this inner action of making holy and the act of setting this sinner apart to belong to the body of Christ and the kingdom of God.

These verbs are probably best seen as a cluster which belong together and which as a whole cluster convey the nature of the human response as well as the richness of the divine initiative and action. We could of course add other verbs to these clusters – e.g. to the first the verbs 'to watch and to pray' and to the second 'to reconcile and to redeem and to save'. And we must remember that the verbs in each cluster always point to what God has done in Jesus Christ, in his life, sacrificial death and glorious exaltation into heaven.

Appendix 3

EXTRA PERSPECTIVES

Obviously conversion can be examined and/or interpreted from a variety of perspectives. Those employed in this book have been theological and historical, concentrating on information taken from the Bible and a variety of written Christian sources. But working within these valid and important perspectives, we need to be aware that the phenomenon we call conversion has been, and remains (especially in North America), a frequent research topic for professionals in the behavioural sciences. The published material in learned articles and books covers a very wide spectrum: e.g. the adoption of Christianity or Islam by whole tribes in Africa or Asia, the 'born-again' experiences of white American teenagers, conversion to Islam of black Americans, and entry into one or another of the weird cults that seem to flourish in California.

It is probably fair to claim that there are very few, if any, assured results in all these studies: however, there are all kinds of suggestive hints and insights. What follows are some points or observations that seem to me to be important, especially for someone who looks at conversion primarily from a biblical, theological or historical perspective.

1. Conversion that is experienced as a crisis has also a process built into it. When recounting how they were converted, many people will emphasise a particular moment for that is what stands out in their memory and feelings. Further, this is often the way in which they believe they ought to understand what has happened to them.

Psychologists who have studied the testimonies of converts to committed Christianity have found that before the crisis experience called conversion the converts were prepared for the possibility of the experience by other preparatory experiences. In teenagers these are usually such things as (a) a sense of dissatisfaction with life; (b) partial involvement with a Christian group/sub-culture – e.g. on a campus of a college; (c) a deeply emotional experience creating a sense of crisis or failure – e.g. through failing examinations or a love-affair going wrong; (d) a hope or belief that religion can solve one's problems; (e) interaction and involvement with people who have strong belief and commitment; and (f) a home background involving church affiliation.

Following the actual 'crisis' or 'encounter', conversion is consolidated through the incorporation into a group, society, or church and this usually includes some form of initiation – e.g. adult baptism or the receiving into membership by the giving of the right hand of fellowship. Thus conversion is a process with a crisis and would not occur without both constituents.

Other psychologists have noted that in those who claim an experience of conversion there was a definite sense of deficiency – that is, something lacking in life, which could be supplied through joining the group or church. The sense of deficit or deficiency can take one of several forms. There is the deficit of social rewards, the experience of not feeling rightly valued or esteemed by the society in which one moves. There is, also, the deficit of consistency of life, the experience of living in a crisis caused by events seemingly outside one's control. Further, there is the deficit of religious solidarity, the experience of being confused about, and lacking clarity, concerning moral and religious values.

Finally, there is the deficit of personal influence, the experience of lacking a close, effective bond with people of strong religious ties. Where a person has two or more of these deficits it seems that she or he is more prepared for religious commitment than others who only have one deficit or none.

It is possible, say other psychologists, to describe conversion as having three parts to it. The first is a period of growing awareness (which will be developing through the experience of a sense of deficit, feelings of dissatisfaction and so on) leading to the realisation that the Christian faith is probably the answer. The second is a period of consideration in which the role of a witness or advocate for the faith is usually important: this could be in person-to-person encounter in an evangelistic meeting or in a small group meeting. Consideration leads to acceptance of the new faith and commitment to it, which itself requires the third stage of incorporation into the society which represents this new faith. Of course, people can drop out at any point in this progression and the time taken, as well as the contributing factors, will be different in each individual case. It is impossible to prove that each person must go through specific preparation: what seems clear is that there is always some form of preparation (which the convert may or may not recognise as such) before genuine commitment in religion: and, further, commitment leads to incorporation into the society of the people of the new faith.

2. Conversion is from one faith to another faith or from one way of relating to a faith to another way of relating to that same faith. Thus conversion to the committed practice of Christian faith can take place from any of the religions of the world (Islam, Hinduism, and so on), from any of the ideologies of the world (atheism, agnosticism, and so on) and from the various forms of secularist materialism and half-belief which are found in the Western world. It always includes accepting new beliefs and values or seeing old beliefs and values in a new perspective. The important point is that everyone has some kind of faith which is either left behind or newly interpreted through conversion.

3. Conversion appears to take place more often during teenage than at any other time in life. This has been noted by many researchers. For example, in his famous study, *The Varieties of Religious Experience*, based on his Gifford Lectures in Scotland of 1901–2, William James wrote:

> In his recent work on the *Psychology of Religion*, Professor E. D. Starbuck of California has shown by a statistical inquiry how closely parallel in its manifestations the ordinary 'conversion' which occurs in young people brought up in evangelical circles is to that growth into a larger spiritual life which is a normal phase of adolescence in every class of human beings. The age is the same, falling usually between fourteen and seventeen. The symptoms are the same – sense of incompleteness and imperfection; brooding, depression, morbid introspection, and sense of sin. And the result is the same – a happy relief and objectivity, as the confidence in self gets greater through the adjustment of the faculties to the wider outlook.

He concluded that 'Starbuck's conclusion . . . would seem to be the only sound one', and added, 'Conversion is in its essence a normal, adolescent phenomenon, incidental to the passage from the child's small universe to the wider, intellectual and spiritual life of maturity.'

If Starbuck and James are followed then conversion is only the resolution of such conflicts as come to the fore during adolescence. This is, of course, to claim too much. What is probably true is that adolescent conversion is an answer to and resolution of identity and sexual conflicts in some – but not all – cases. We need to remember that conversion may also be related to other periods of change or stress in life – e.g. the so-called mid-life crisis. If all this is admitted, it is still possible to assert that conversion is actually more than the solution to the crisis, and that in some cases conversion is not actually specifically related to the major crises of adolescence.

4. *Certain personality types are not predisposed to particular types or forms of conversion. Further, the change which is involved in conversion is not a change of personality.* We are all aware that it is not easy to define personality for it is not directly observable; its existence is established by inference from variation in a person's behaviour, and it points to that which gives a person consistency from situation to situation through time. Personality refers to those internal qualities which define individual personhood and which make individual differences evident.

William James spent a lot of time in his Gifford Lectures dealing with the personality traits of those whom he called the 'once-born' and the 'twice-born' and he believed that only certain types of personality (the 'sick souls', with, for example, a psychopathic temperament) needed an experience of conversion. Others, following in his footsteps, have claimed that people who need to undergo a deep conversion experience are usually from the less-intelligent members of the population and also more subject to hysteria. But more recent study appears to show that it is impossible to prove either that the form that conversion takes is directly related to particular personality types or that, specifically, the neurotic and anxious person needs a 'sudden conversion'!

In *Psychology of Christian Conversion* (1969), Robert O. Ferm claims that conversion does cause a radical change in personality. This book has a preface by Billy Graham and its whole orientation is towards the idea that conversion is a crisis experience resulting in a great change, wherein a 'new creature' is formed. If true, this would be a great boost to the claims made on behalf of evangelistic crusades and instantaneous, marvellous conversion. But Ferm's claims have not been verified by serious research: rather conversion is seen to be more about a change in direction of life, together with changes in values and ideas, rather than in the essence of personality.

5. The changes achieved through psychotherapy are not to be confused with conversion. It is well known that various positive changes can be gained through psychotherapy. These include mental health and stability, better interpersonal relationships and self-realisation/self-actualisation (which involves having meaningful and worth-while goals). However, it is possible to become a changed person who denies the need for conversion in the religious sense since psychotherapy can be merely related to living meaningfully in terms of totally secularist values. Yet, in some cases, it is possible that psychotherapy paves the way for the felt need for conversion. On the other hand, it is quite possible that a person just converted actually needs psychotherapy since conversion does not imply wholeness but the beginnings of a journey of sanctification towards wholeness!

6. The testimony of the convert, expressed in spoken or written word, is not usually the raw report of his/her experience, but is a report which combines personal experience with the theology, symbolism and particular religious language of the group which the person has joined. To claim this is in no way to accuse converts of being deceitful; but it is to state that most people interpret what has happened to them in terms compatible with the views of members of the group to which they belong. They do this without particularly thinking about it. I have particularly noticed this phenomenon when visiting the USA from England. Usually I go to various types of evangelical churches and colleges as well as Anglican churches of a traditional as well as Charismatic type. The Lutherans tend to be dominated by language based on the distinction between 'Law and Gospel', while the Calvinists tend to be dominated by 'effectual and sovereign grace' and the revivalistic fundamentalists by 'following, talking to and listening to Jesus'. Anglican talk is much more sacramentalist and, except where it is Charismatic, hesitant to speak openly of personal, religious experience. Conversion seems to occur for Lutherans in a Lutheran way, for Calvinists in a

Calvinist way and for revivalists in a revivalist way! The Calvinist is much more likely to speak of 'the Lord opening my eyes' and the revivalist to speak of 'I realised that . . .' than the other way round. And where Calvinists and revivalists are prone to say 'Christ' or 'Lord' the Lutherans will say 'Gospel' – e.g. 'commitment to the Gospel'.

7. *Life-changing conversions to other faiths than Christianity occur.* There are, for example, many Black Muslims in the USA who testify to a real change in their lives when they became Muslims. Not a few robbers, drug-addicts, murderers and rapists have been changed into law-abiding and God-fearing citizens. Then there are many who have become Mormons or Jehovah's Witnesses whose life style and belief systems have dramatically changed. Books could be filled with testimonies to the changes brought about through conversion to a major religion (e.g. Islam and Buddhism) or a sect/cult (e.g. Mormonism and the Unification Church).

Keen evangelical Christians are prone to explain such conversions as the work of Satan, who seeks to simulate or imitate everything that Christ does. Such a claim is debatable. What is much clearer is that at both the social and psychological level people are definitely changed when they leave the Westernised half-belief in God for a definite belief offered by a major religion or cult. Socially, they change their behaviour, gain new friends and fellowship and pursue different activities and goals. At the inner level they testify to new contentment, peace, purpose and commitment. They speak of a new relationship with God which gives them a sense of identity and purpose.

A lot of the interesting work in research into religious conversion has been done with respect to the turning of young Americans to the cults of Eastern and Western origin. Whatever else this research has revealed it has shown that genuine conversions – in terms of life-changing experiences – do occur.

8. What distinguishes and differentiates one conversion from another is not the psychosocial process but the actual content. For example, the turning of a person from half-belief (in God and secularism) to orthodox Christianity or to join the Moonies or to become a Mormon is much the same in terms of sociological and psychological observation and investigation. What distinguishes the one from the other are the different beliefs and values adopted, and societies joined.

This point has been made very clearly and forcibly by J. Harold Ellens. He builds upon the teaching of James W. Fowler in his influential *Stages of Faith* (1981), and sees the phenomenon of conversion in this manner:

> When a person experiences a significant new life-shaping insight, relationship or trauma, that event-experience cuts down through all the structures and defence processes of the personality structure or developmental formation and reaches all the way down to the characterological level. There, at that level, the cognitive, psychosocial and moral-spiritual content of the 'significant emotional event' produces a paradigm shift in the value and belief system. The assumptions, commitments, 'loves', values or beliefs which have here-to-fore constituted the ground of being and integrating perspective are now all illumined in a new way with the new light of the 'new, significant event of the psyche'.

To illustrate what he has in mind, Ellens refers to the shift in the visual pattern in a kaleidoscope as you turn the barrel two or more degrees. So also at the level of the psyche, the shift or turn in experience produces an alteration in the internal system of believing and valuing. As there is no change in the basic nature of the crystals in the kaleidoscope, so also there is no basic change in personality. Yet everything seems to have become different.

Here is how Ellens describes Christian conversion as a 'significant, emotional event'.

> It involves a new personal relationship with God in Christ, a new insight regarding the truth about God and self, and a new

trauma as one is confronted with an entirely new world of moral claim, ontological reality, and vocational destiny. Frequently Christian conversion involves all three kinds of events in conjunction. Sometimes the conversion starts in trauma; moral, physical or psychical; and then moves through new insight to a new relationship. At other times it starts with a new relationship, often mediated through a new quality of human relationship, and moves on, therefore, to new insight and the new trauma of personality reintegration. At still other times it starts in new insights and grows to include the other two factors. Sometimes it takes place mainly on only one of the three levels.

However, he holds that conversion to Judaism or Islam or a cult happens in much the same way: psychodynamically and sociodynamically there is no difference – or at least no major difference. Whether or not this apparent fact requires us to state the following with Ellens is another question: 'The work of the Holy Spirit, the phenomena of Christian conversion, and the dynamics of our transforming moments are no more supernatural than the formation of coal under the physicochemical laws of hydrocarbons under pressure.'

What orthodox Christians normally claim is that Christian conversion is a turning to God in response to his call, which may be heard, felt and received in a variety of ways and means. The *responding* person is a thinking person and so there will be changes of mind concerning God, self and sin in the act or process of turning. He or she is a *feeling* person and so there will be mild or intense feelings of grief, guilt and conflict; also he or she is a *deciding* person and so there will be a definite exercise of will to follow Christ and submit to God's will. Observation of the cognitive, affective and decision-making processes can be made, we have seen, by behavioural scientists. What they cannot predict or describe is the secret, inward and invisible divine action and intervention. However, if the results of this inward, divine activity are instantaneously obvious in the attitude and actions of the *responding* person then their observations will include those results.

The discussion of conversion in this appendix has been of that type which occurs in adolescence or later and includes a definite crisis as part of a longer process of turning from one faith to another.

Further, a disadvantage – perhaps a major one – in the findings into the psychosocial process of conversion is that they do not cover observation of conversion in a genuine revival. Unlike Jonathan Edwards, the philosopher-theologian of New England in the eighteenth century, who observed and reflected upon the phenomenon of conversion during a period of intense religious awakening and revival (see his *Treatise on the Religious Affections*), modern behavioural scientists have not been able to be present in such a revival.

In times of revival there is not only an abundance of scripturally-based preaching and teaching but also a great stirring of the emotions. People do not merely feel a sense of failure and lacking a purpose in life, they also have very intense feelings about their relationship to God. They feel guilty as sinners because they have personally offended Almighty God, the judge: they feel that their sins are so immense as to be beyond forgiveness: they see the sacrificial atonement of Christ as their only plea before God for grace and pardon: they know that without Christ as their Saviour they face the prospect of the divine wrath and the punishment of hell. They feel that only a visitation by the divine Spirit into their hearts will enable them to repent and believe as God requires.

And after they have been drawn into true faith, they feel that a massive burden has been lifted from their hearts: they know that the cloud that blocked their communion with God has been removed in and by Christ their mediator and their hearts are filled with new and powerful emotions –

love of God and his excellence, joy in the eternal salvation in which they share, a sense of peace within and a great desire to tell others that God has forgiven, accepted and blessed them.

Certainly studies have been made by psychologists of the written testimonies of people converted in revivals; but, studying accounts is not the same as being present in a revival and studying living people. Further, since very few modern-day converts appear to feel an overwhelming sense of the holiness of God and their own sin, it is difficult (if not impossible) to study anything like the revival phenomenon of conversion today. Thus the intriguing question as to whether a pre-conversion experience of a great weight and guilt of sin is only a phenomenon of a period of revival (and, perhaps, of earlier centuries in the West) remains open.

BIBLIOGRAPHY

A. Anthropology

Costas, Orlando E., 'Conversion as a complex experience', *Gospel in Context*, 1 (1978), pp. 14ff.

Hesselgrave, D. J., *Communicating Christ Cross-Culturally* (Zondervan, Grand Rapids, 1978).

Horton, R., 'On the rationality of conversion', *Africa*, 45 (1975), pp. 219ff., 373ff.

Kraft, C. H., *Christianity in Culture* (Orbis, Maryknoll, New York, 1979).

Mayers, M. K., *Christianity confronts culture* (Zondervan, Grand Rapids, 1974).

Tippett, A. R., 'Conversion as a dynamic process in Christian mission', *Missiology*, 2 (1977), pp. 203ff.

Wallace, A. F. C., 'Revitalization Movements', *American Anthropologist*, 58 (1956), pp. 264ff.

B. Biblical Theology

Barclay, William, *Turning to God: a study of conversion in the Book of Acts* (Westminster Press, Philadelphia, 1964).

Goppelt, Leonhard, *Theology of the New Testament*, vol. 1 (Wm. B. Eerdmans, Grand Rapids, 1981).

Guthrie, Donald, *New Testament Theology* (Inter-Varsity Press, Leicester, 1981).

Jeremias, Joachim, *New Testament Theology*, vol. 1 (S.C.M. Press, London, 1971).

Kümmel, W. G., *The Theology of the New Testament* (Abingdon Press, Nashville, 1973).

Manson, T. W., *The Teaching of Jesus* (Cambridge University Press, 1963).

New International Dictionary of New Testament Theology, 3 vols, ed. Colin Brown (Paternoster Press, Exeter, 1975–8). Articles on 'conversion' and 'repentance'.

Smalley, S. S., 'Conversion in the New Testament', *The Churchman*, vol. 78 (1964), pp. 193ff.

C. Historical Theology

(i) primary texts

Augustine, *Confessions*, trans. E. M. Blaiklock (Thomas Nelson, Nashville, 1983).

Baxter, Richard, *Practical Works* (Baker Book House, Grand Rapids, 1981). In this volume are various books on conversion.

Book of Concord: *The Confessions of the Evangelical Lutheran Church*, trans. T. G. Tapper (Fortress Press, Philadelphia, 1959). This contains the Catechisms of Luther and the Formula of Concord.

Book of Common Prayer (1549, 1552, 1662).

Calvin, John, *The Institutes of the Christian Religion*, ed. J. T. McNeill, trans. F. L. Battles, 2 vols (Westminster Press, Philadelphia, 1960).

Conversions: the Christian Experience, eds H. T. Kerr and J. M. Mulder (Hodder & Stoughton, London, 1984). This contains the accounts of the conversions of Augustine, Calvin, Wesley, Whitefield, Edwards, Brainerd, Finney and others: each account is taken from the original source.

Cyprian, *Ad Donatum* (Letter to Donatus), in his *Letters*, 2 vols (Edinburgh, 1869).

Documents of the Baptismal Liturgy, ed. E. C. Whitaker (S.P.C.K., London, 1960). This contains the Apostolic Tradition of Hippolytus and other texts.

Dort, Canons of, trans. A. A. Hoekema (*Calvin Theological Journal*, Grand Rapids, 1968).

Finney, C. G., *Lectures on Systematic Theology* (E. J. Goodrich, Oberlin, 1878).

Vatican II: the Conciliar and Post Conciliar Documents, ed. Austin Flannery, O.P. (Fowler Wright Ltd, Leominster, 1981). This contains the *Decree on Missionary Activity*.

Wesley, John, *Journal*, ed. N. Curnock (Eaton & Mains, New York, 1909).

Wesley, John, *Forty-Four Sermons* (Epworth Press, London, 1944).

Whitefield, George, *Journals* (Banner of Truth, Edinburgh, 1960).

Whitefield, George, *Sermons*, ed. John Gillies (Middletown, 1837). This selection contains the sermon on Zacchaeus.

(ii) secondary texts

Burnish, R., *The Meaning of Baptism: a comparison of the teaching and practice of the Fourth Century with the present day* (S.P.C.K., London, 1985).

Brauer, J. C., 'Conversion: from Puritanism to Revivalism', *Journal of Religion*, 58, pp. 227ff.

Green, Michael, *Evangelism in the Early Church* (Hodder & Stoughton, London, 1970).

Nock, A. D., *Conversion* (Oxford University Press, 1933).

Nock, A. D., 'Conversion and Adolescence', in *Arthur Darby Nock: Essays*, ed. Z. Stewart (Harvard University Press, 1972).

Pettit, N., *The Heart Prepared: Grace and Conversion in Puritan Spiritual Life* (Yale University Press, 1966).

Leclercq, Jean, *The Love of Learning and the Desire for God: a study of monastic culture* (S.P.C.K., London, 1978).

D. Psychology

Ellens, J. H., 'The Psychodynamics of Christian Conversion', in *Journal of Psychology and Christianity*, vol 3, no. 4, pp. 29ff.

Ferm, Robert O., *Psychology of Christian Conversion* (1969).

Fowler, James W., *Stages of Faith: the psychology of human development* (Harper & Row, New York, 1981).

Gillespie, V. B., *Religious Conversion and Personal Identity* (Religious Education Press, Birmingham, Al., 1979).

James, W., *The Varieties of Religious Experience* (Longmans, Green & Co., London, 1928).

Johnson, C. B., and Malony, H. N., *Christian Conversion: biblical and psychological perspectives* (Zondervan, Grand Rapids, 1982).

Roberts, F. J., 'Some psychological factors in religious conversion', *British Journal of Social and Clinical Psychology*, 4 (1978), pp. 185ff.

E. Sociology

Beckford, J. A., 'Accounting for Conversion', *British Journal of Sociology*, 29, pp. 249ff.

Heinrich, Max, 'Change of Heart: A test of some widely held theories about religious conversion', *American Journal of Sociology*, 83 (1977), pp. 653ff.

Taylor, B., 'Conversion and Cognition: an area for empirical study in the microsociology of religious knowledge', *Social Compass*, 23 (1976), pp. 5ff.

Taylor, B., 'Recollection and Membership: converts' talk and the ratiocination of commonality', *Sociology*, 12 (1978), pp. 316ff.

Wimberley, R. C., 'Conversion in a Billy Graham Crusade: spontaneous event of ritual performance', *Sociological Quarterly*, 16 (1975), pp. 162ff.

F. *Theology*

Barth, K., 'The Awakening to Conversion', in *Church Dogmatics*, vol. 4:2 (T. & T. Clark, Edinburgh, 1958).

Conversion: perspectives on personal and social transformation (Alba House, New York, 1978).

Graham, Billy, 'The New Birth', in *Fundamentals of the Faith*, ed. C. F. H. Henry (Zondervan, Grand Rapids, 1969).

Helm, Paul, *The Beginnings: Word and Spirit in Conversion* (Banner of Truth Trust, Edinburgh, 1986).

Newbigin, Leslie, *The Finality of Christ* (John Knox Press, Atlanta, 1969).

Stott, J. R. W., *Christian Mission in the Modern World* (Kingsway Publications, Eastbourne, 1985).

Wallis, Jim, *The Call to Conversion* (Harper & Row, New York, 1982).

Weinandy, Thomas, *Receiving the Promise: the Spirit's work in conversion* (The Word among us Press, Washington, D.C., 1985).